6/23

I hope this will inspire you to
do likewise!

Marsha Williams.

18.5.87-

Exiled to America

Also by Masha Williams
White Among the Reds (Shepheard-Walwyn)
The Consul's Memsahib (The Book Guild Ltd.)

Exiled to America

Masha Williams

The Book Guild Ltd
Sussex England

The Book Guild Ltd
25 High Street,
Lewes, Sussex

First published 1987
© Masha Williams 1987

Set in Linotron Cartier
Typeset by CST, Eastbourne
Printed in Great Britain by
Antony Rowe Ltd
Chippenham, Wilts

ISBN 0 86332 234 4

1

"Look Alan!" and I nudged my husband. "That priest over there is making the Sign of the Cross with a lighted cigarette!"

"Sh!" he whispered. "They can hear you."

"They can't. They're miles away."

But to my embarrassment the priest stubbed out his cigarette. The others with him put down their cigars. They straightened up in their chairs, lowered their voices and some glanced surreptitiously my way.

It was 1950 and we were speeding towards New York. There I would be the wife of the British Deputy Consul-General. Such a mouthful! But that was days away and meanwhile, never having been to the States, I could not help peering at these priests, so obviously American, in their brightly-coloured check shirts. They had crossed themselves with sweeping gestures before sitting down to breakfast at the opposite end of the dining-saloon. They lit up fat cigars and their hearty voices resounded above the low-toned conversations of the British.

"See? They heard you," Alan murmured. "It's the echo. Ships have strange ways with sound. For goodness sake, be careful!" and he retreated behind the ship's newspaper, only his fair, curly hair showing above it, his large solid figure a stern rebuke. I tried not to laugh and after whispering, "I've always thought Americans vulgar," I fell silent.

The storms had subsided and though the Caronia was still rolling, we managed breakfast and I felt light-hearted.

"Come! Let's explore the ship," and I seized Alan's hand. We were travelling with our two children, Libet and Lawrence, Mamoo, as we all called my mother, and Mary, our Irish nanny. The children came running up, relieved to see us on our feet again. Libet clung to our hands grinning up at us, a plump little girl, nearly three, with a big white bow on the fair, almost white curls, that tumbled down to her shoulders. Lawrence ran ahead. He was nearly two, a slight but sturdy figure with the same rosy cheeks and fair hair. Mary was still prostrated on her bed.

I revelled in the luxury of the Caronia, in our First Class cabin with its twin beds, dressing tables and a wardrobe. No more sitting on a hard bench, as I used to when I crossed the Channel before I married into the Foreign Service.

In the Games Room we discovered the clergy playing bridge, and for money. Gambling! I was so shocked I stood staring at them speechless, but they appeared unconcerned. Later on deck we met them striding along in flamboyant tartan check caps, and I had to laugh in spite of myself. The British wore dark tweed headgear, and Alan was bare-headed.

"Hot from Rome, they must think they can afford these indulgences," he smiled and then added, "But perhaps they're merely trying to show what 'regular fellows' they are."

Tea, a solemn occasion, was taken daily in the spacious, high-ceilinged lounge. Seated in soft leather armchairs at round tables covered with spotless, damask cloths, passengers spoke in whispers as they handed each other the thinnest slices of bread and butter. White-jacketed waiters glided noiselessly over the thick carpet. The passengers all looked alike, the women in twin-sets over tweed skirts with a single string of pearls and the men in sports jackets and grey flannels with a discreet tie.

"Why are the British First Class passengers such a dull lot?" I sighed.

Alan raised his eyebrows. "You can't have it both ways, Americans vulgar and the British boring."

Outside the windows I could see the whole world sparkling in the sunshine. I left Alan with his Times and rushed out. Mamoo was standing with the children at the rails, head held chin up into the wind, bracing her comfortable figure against it. Lawrence kept burying his face in her skirts, shouting, "Peep-oh!" as Libet groped her way round Mamoo's legs, and grabbed him with a "Gotcher!" Both were convulsed with laughter. Mamoo's skirts were tugged this way and that, but she let the children play. How lucky we are to have her with us, I thought. Joining them, I breathed in the heady, salt air. We watched the big waves crashing against the side of the ship, rising up its side, and we laughed as spray showered over us.

"Look children, America!" I cried. A thin line had appeared on the horizon. We watched as it thickened and suddenly Mamoo pointed to a tiny island with square buildings.

"There's Ellis Island. I was interned there." She fell silent and went on stroking Lawrence's head.

"Interned! Why? When was this?"

"You wouldn't remember. You were a child." I stared at her in astonishment. She did not believe in complaining, but never to mention such an experience!

"Tell me about it," I urged.

"It's nothing. Your father was ill and I came over to nurse him. He was unable to meet me and I was taken there."

My family were Russian refugees and stateless. My father left us in England when he went to the States, hoping, mistakenly as it turned out, to make money and bring us all over. That was many years ago.

Mamoo went on, "I was lonely that first night lying on my bunk, and very frightened. I didn't know what lay ahead. Then suddenly I heard the familiar jingle of a cross and little ikons. I sat up, and imagine! In the bunk opposite was a lady with a gold cross and a bunch of silver ikons round her neck, just like mine. 'I'm Russian too!' I cried, jumping down. We embraced and became friends, and from then on it wasn't too bad. We kept together till your father was able to fetch me." She gazed, suddenly sad, at the horizon. My father had died.

"It's chilly. I'll take the children down; it's their supper time." She was smiling again and taking their hands, she led them away.

I stared at the land ahead. The United States! The New World! The Caronia was heading towards the Statue of Liberty, and passengers now crowded the deck. The setting sun played over the gigantic figure brandishing the Torch of Freedom and supposedly welcoming refugees. But were the States still hospitable and welcoming? Not towards poor Mamoo. As we sped past the statue, the stern features and the spikes encircling the head looked forbidding. I wrapped my fur coat tighter round me.

The battery loomed up. New York! Sharp-cornered square

New York

blocks shooting up into the sky. Soon we were steaming up the Hudson River. Enormous buildings towered above us. I felt insignificant, puny, as I clutched the hand-rail. I was about to become 'official', a British representative, but I wasn't prepared. I hadn't been given instructions or information, and Alan had only warned me that 'socialising' would be my job. That wasn't exactly my line . . . I longed for the security of those familiar twin-sets and the single string of pearls.

The Caronia was swinging round towards her berth. She hooted long and loud. Tugs whistled, the noise was deafening. It might frighten the children. I hurried down.

Libet was sobbing on her bunk, "Naughty whistle!" her pudgy hands over her ears. I held her soft little body till she stopped crying and fell asleep. Lawrence slept on, arms above his head, fists clenched. Both were already in their long brown corduroy trousers. Mary was stuffing clothes into a suit-case. Her normally pink and white cheeks were almost grey. She had dark patches under her big blue eyes and she no longer smiled.

"It's all over now, Mary. We've arrived."

"I want to go home . . ." Her mouth hung open. Tears were on her long dark lashes. I helped her fasten the case. Alan was locking our hand-luggage. Suit-cases, parcels and export packages were strewn over the floor.

A knock on the door. It was Mamoo. "Can I come in? I've brough my bags." Alan took them from her.

"That makes twenty-three pieces. And that's only our hand-luggage," he said irritably, but Mamoo only smiled and leant over Lawrence, covering him with a rug. He was her special grandchild. Then she noticed Mary.

"My poor dear! Yes, the sea has been rough, but I never missed a meal." She laughed. "Nor did the Captain, but the waiters, how they rushed us through the courses. They felt sick, poor things."

The phone rang.

"That's it. We're landing," Alan announced. Mamoo hurried to put Lawrence's jacket and woollen cap on him, while Mary dressed Libet. The children slept on. A ship's officer appeared.

"The gang-plank is down, Sir. Please follow me. We'll see to your luggage." Alan's expression was stern as he picked up his

Alan and myself on board RMS Queen Mary

heavy, bulging brief-case (he never let it out of his hands) and we followed the officer, Mamoo and Mary carrying the sleeping children snug in their arms. My heart was beating fast. I was perspiring. Could I hold on to Alan's arm? No, it would not do. The deck was a solid mass of families, straining towards the gang-plank which was corded off on both sides. Children whined, parents stumbled over suit-cases, everyone was leaden with too many parcels. The officer led us down. I took a deep breath and stifled the sickly feeling welling up inside me. I was no longer just myself, a private individual; as I stepped on to American soil, I became the wife of the British Deputy Consul-General.

2

In the vast, crowded customs shed, I hovered nervously in the background while consular officials, all sombrely dressed, dealt with our twenty-three pieces of luggage. The bustle and brilliant lights had woken the children and, shrieking with laughter, they chased each other between the luggage counters while Mary called urgently,

"Libet! Lawrence! Come back!"

Suddenly, behind a glass partition I recognised my brother, Vania. I rushed across and a policeman raised a barrier for me.

"Hi, Masha!" he shouted. I had not seen him for twenty-five years. That last time Mamoo, my sisters and I had stood tearful on Victoria Station as Vania, a slim, awkward youth, peered sadly from the train window. He waved both arms as the train started and he went on waving till it swung round a corner and he disappeared, off to join his father and to seek better luck in the States. It was the only time I saw Mamoo cry and my face crinkled up too.

And now I was being kissed and hugged by this tall, heavy, broad-shouldered man with thinning hair and blue eyes behind steel-rimmed glasses, a statistician in a Wall Street broker's firm.

"You're nearly as tall as I!" he exclaimed and we laughed, at nothing, just at being together. I noticed a red and white checked flannel shirt under his grey wind-jacket, and the thought flickered through my mind — hardly formal wear. What is he thinking of? But I forgot my embarrassment as I gazed up at the boyish grin sweeping away the stern lines on his face. I clung to his arm, though I felt shy; so many years separated us and I had acquired British reserve. I was glad when the children ran up.

"This is Uncle Vania," I told them. Vania's right eyebrow shot up crookedly — a familiar, endearing gesture. His hands dived into his jacket pockets and out came two bars of chocolate. The children pounced on them.

"Uncle Chocolate!" Lawrence cried and Uncle Chocolate he became. I remembered the bars of chocolate Vania used to hide in our trunks when we sisters were packed off, sobbing miserably, to boarding school. How comforting they had been.

"Here's Katia!" he said and there was my eldest sister, whom I had not seen for several years either. She was married to a Russian-American and lived in New York. She tripped along, elegant in black silk and as handsome as ever, with big grey eyes and pitch black hair, parted down the middle. Like Mamoo she wore no make-up. 'Muck', Alan called it. He would like her, I felt sure. I was wearing a lavender tweed costume, the only one I had with me and such a contrast to her outfit, but I thought nothing of it.

"Hullo, Masha!" and, reserved as ever, she laid her cheek against mine. "Hullo, darlings," and she kissed the tops of the children's heads.

Alan joined us, his first meeting with his in-laws. I watched anxiously. He glanced quickly at them, smiled, kissed Katia and shook Vania's hand. He laughed at Vania's greeting, "Hi, Alan!"

"It's marvellous to have a brother and sister ready-made," he said, and obviously meant it. I pressed his arm. Mamoo and Mary came up with the loaded trolleys.

"Vanichka!" Mamoo cried as he kissed her. "My dearest Katiousha!" My sister smiled and allowed herself to be kissed. Mamoo travelled back and forth to the States and had been seeing them regularly, but every time was a special joy. Mary shook hands, blushing and shy.

We piled into a consular car that was to take us to the Stanhope Hotel. Vania and Katia drove behind us. I looked eagerly out of the window, my first glimpse of New York. It was night now. Dim, narrow streets and then we were suddenly in Fifth Avenue, the centre of the city, dividing it in two. We crawled along through the heavy traffic, brilliant coloured lights flashing all round and the wail of sirens deafening. The pavements were crammed with people forging ahead in both directions, looking neither to right nor left, like ants, I thought, and all in such a hurry. I shall never be able to keep up with them!

At last the hotel. Inside, our feet sank into thick carpets. The white hall with its gilded chandeliers and damask-covered couches and arm-chairs was entirely suitable for the Deputy C-G (Consul-General), but not for his children, and I sighed; it's the double life again, public and private and so difficult to reconcile. The uniformed doorman kept edging nearer Alan, who frowned till he realised the man was waiting for his tip. The receptionist hurried forward, the uniformed staff stared at us. As from now we're in the public eye, I thought, and it was as if a weight suddenly pressed down on me, a physical sensation. But there was nothing to be done; I had to live with it. It was strange that Alan seemed immune; he must be used to it.

We shot up in the elevator to a three-roomed suite on the seventh floor. The liftman clung to Alan till he got his tip. Alan glared at his back.

"Do I have to tip every time we go in and out?" he asked.

"Yes, every one of them and all the time," Vania laughed.

Katia gave Libet a brightly-coloured jigsaw puzzle and Lawrence a wooden train. "To keep them occupied while we help you unpack and settle in." How considerate she is, I thought gratefully.

Once the children were in bed and the door closed on them and Mary, Vania ordered a night-cap. "And I'll do the tipping," he chuckled.

But Mary was crying. I went in to her. The bed-clothes were half on the floor, her face was in the pillow and her plump shoulders heaved. "I want to go home," she sobbed.

"You'll feel better in the morning, dear." I pulled up the bed-clothes and tucked her in. You're lonely, Mary, I thought, and I'm scared. I'd like to tell Vania and Katia; they're kind, but I'm official so I can't. I must be strong. I kissed the back of her head and closed the door softly.

Katia looked up. "The Police are all Irish here. She'll meet them and she's so pretty, she'll make friends easily. There'll be other nannies in the park too."

When Vania and Katia left with Mamoo who was to sleep at Katia's till we found a flat, Alan and I hurried to the window and drew back the curtains. Below lay the darkness of Central Park, criss-crossed with streaks of light as cars raced up its roads, and beyond the trees, millions of tiny squares of yellow light, piled on top of each other, up and up into the sky. I clutched Alan's arm and we stood close to each other.

"It's fascinating," I murmured, but I did not admit how frightening it was too.

Next morning Mary was beaming. We had missed supper the night before, so we tucked into cereals, eggs, bacon, toast, coffee, with milk for the children, all conveniently wheeled in on trolleys. We were laughing, carefree after a good night's sleep, when the bill arrived and a string of waiters expecting tips.

"I don't have that amount of dollars," Alan exclaimed, "and I can't get more till the end of the month."

"There's nothing we can do," I said. "We've eaten it all!" Strange that the Foreign Office did not seem to realise that we had to eat. Katia was with us. She had undertaken to accompany Mary and the children to the Park while we reported to the Consulate. She now suggested, "You'd better eat in drug-stores."

"At the chemist's?" I was amazed.

"Yes. They're much cheaper." Katia must know so we decided to try them.

As we left I asked for two cots. The children were not safe in beds without sides.

The Consulate was on Fifth Avenue at 34th Street, in the Empire State Building, and on the 61st floor! I could not imagine it, right up in the sky, a terrifying prospect as I hate heights. We took a single-decker long green bus down Fifth Avenue. Passengers sat on either side facing each other. The women are so dolled up, I thought. A thin, elderly lady opposite me was a symphony in brilliant mauve from the frivolous nest of pompoms and veiling on her hair down to the tip of her spiky shoes. Vivid rouge on her cheeks, mascara on her eyelashes, her whole face concealed under make-up, she wore an expressionless mask or so it seemed to me, coming from post-war drab London. What is she really like, I wondered. She can't be as hard as she looks. Silly, those childish pompoms on her head. I looked round at the other women.

11

Their faces were camouflaged too. They're taking on false personalities. What a strain! And why? Are they afraid to be themselves? Alan's colleagues posted to New York had told us how thrilling it was to be among smartly-dressed women, and with a pang of jealousy, I told myself that we didn't have the time to give so much thought to appearances. But how would I get along with such women?

"We're there." Alan got up as the bus hissed to a stop. On the pavement, buffeted by hurrying crowds we searched for the Empire State Building. All we saw was an endless line of shop fronts, surmounted by buildings towering over us. Alan, a stickler for punctuality, grumbled, "It's already nine-thirty. Where is the darned building?"

"Why not ask someone?" But he would not. So we chased up and down the street. When he was looking the other way I asked a doorman. "Where's the Empire State Building?" Solemnly he pointed a forefinger skywards. The building in front rose up and up and disappeared into the sky, its tip invisible. The Empire State Building.

Grinning foolishly we pushed through the swing doors past all the people rushing out, and were faced with rows of groups of elevators, covering different sets of floors. Finally we found lifts serving floors 56 to 67. We squeezed into one, stood facing the doors, packed in like so many robots, and whizzed up at terrifying speed to the 61st floor. We got out, my head whirling, and Alan stepped briskly into the Consulate. I hung back trying to compose myself, for the building seemed to be swaying. Then I followed.

A long hall, men and women turning from their counters to stare at us, the new Deputy C-G and his wife. How to get past, I wondered anxiously. They know who I am. They're too numerous to greet individually and I can't bow to right and left like royalty? Feeling extremely self-conscious, I stared ahead, rushed after Alan and into his office. The room was strictly functional — a massive desk, heavy desk-chair, filing cabinets and two deep leather armchairs.

Alan had to meet the C-G, Sir Francis Evans, so he left me with a Mrs Hinkler, a member of the locally-engaged staff, and obviously English; she wore hardly any make-up and dressed soberly and neatly. She smiled and led me to the window.

"Mrs Williams, come and look at this first."

I gasped. In the far, far distance below, miles and miles of square and oblong roofs of all sizes, an occasional spire amongst them, and a maze of narrow parallel lines — streets with minute cars crawling along. I could see right down to the entrance to New York harbour. The city is at my feet, I thought, and I'm on top of the world. A childish delight filled me.

"It's magnificent!" I exclaimed and turned beaming to Mrs Hinkler. "I wonder how much work Alan will do facing such a view."

Then I looked straight down and stepped hurriedly back. It was a sash window about 2'10" from the floor, the bottom half open with only a flimsy piece of glass, deflecting the air upwards into the room, to stop you falling out. Mrs Hinkler remarked, "It's very useful. When I have difficult assistance cases and anyone threatens suicide, I just open the window and show them how easy it is to carry out their threat. It has a sobering effects." Her gentle smile belied the cynical words.

Alan was back. "We're to lunch with the Evanses in the Rainbow Room at the top of the Rockefeller Center. It's a huge complex on Fifth Avenue covering 47th to 51st streets. You go home now and join me there at one. Look upwards or you'll miss it," and he laughed. "Can you find your way back to the hotel?"

"Yes, straight up Fifth Avenue to 81st Street." How easy with all the streets straight and numbered. The Rainbow Room! The Rockefeller Center! It all seemed unreal, exciting. Lunch up in the sky! My heart beat fast.

3

I walked up Fifth Avenue towards the bus stop, peering into the huge shop fronts at the lavish display of an overwhelming assortment of clothes and I nearly fell over a wheel-chair. There seemed to be wheel-chairs everywhere, and cripples on crutches or limping with sticks. I tried to avoid them and to control the sickly feeling welling up inside me but at every street corner women rattled tins labelled 'Fight Polio'. It brought the full horror closer. We had been inoculated against polio before coming to the USA but I had not realised the extent of the epidemic. I hurried on.

On either side enormous buildings towered over me. They blocked out the sky, pressed down, pinned me in. I felt trapped, dwarfed and I panicked. A bus hissed to a stop and I ran for it. I sat down and only managed to pull myself together when the buildings gave way to the trees of Central Park and I breathed freely again.

Back in our hotel suite, I sank into an armchair. So many emotions all in one morning and so many fears to overcome. The children, bursting in and clambering over me, were a relief.

"Wasn't elphant!" Libet shouted.

"No! No! Isn't elphant" Lawrence shook his head.

Katia laughed. "They expected the elephant in the park zoo to be tiny like it is in their picture book." We washed the children's faces and hands. Then Mamoo and Mary took them off to lunch in a drug-store. When they had left, Katia turned to me. "Look, Masha, you can't wear this costume. (I was still in my lavender tweed). New Yorkers wear dark clothes after Labour Day, and no-one wears wool. Rooms are oveheated and it just isn't done." All that money and those clothes coupons wasted and it had looked so smart in London.

"I'll get something dark as soon as I can," I promised, noting

Mamoo and Katia,
my mother and elder
sister

her open,
high-heeled shoes.
I was wearing
walking shoes. I
could never be as
elegant as she is, I
thought, even if
Alan wasn't short
of dollars; it's a
gift, and I don't
have it.

Two extra
camp beds stood
in the children's
room. Strange!
Again I asked for
cots. Then I
climbed into a bus and, with trepidation, was carried back among the sky-scrapers.

The Rockefeller Center however was not oppressive. It was magnificent. Though giant square buildings thrust parallel lines of concrete and glass up into the sky, below in open spaces fountains played amidst multi-coloured flower beds; flags waved gaily over a skating rink and a golden Prometheus sparkled in the sunlight. Down here below it's for modest folk like myself, while the concrete blocks in the sky are for the wizards of finance and power. A clock struck one. Brushing aside my fantasies, I hurried past the mightly Atlas balancing the world on his rippling shoulders and went in. I shot up to the sixty-fifth floor.

Sir Francis, Lady Evans and Alan were on the landing outside the Rainbow Room. They greeted me warmly. The doorman sprang forward and the head waiter hurried up, smiling. Sir Francis was evidently a welcome customer. We were ushered in. There were other guests but I hardly noticed them, for the

Rainbow Room was crowded with New York's smartest set, women in black sheen with dashes of white at neck and wrists, flashes of costume jewelry, and black creations on their costly perms. With the click of bracelets, they gestured gracefully over the tables. Their painted faces looked fresh and youthful in that shadowy light. They filled the low-ceilinged room with a loud buzz of conversation. As I sat down I realised what a country bumkin I must look.

"Welcome, Mrs Williams, to New York," Sir Francis leant towards me. "I hope you will be happy here. I'm sure you will; it's a marvellous place." How distinguished he looked, his grey suit well pressed, shirt gleaming white, gold cuff-links at his slender wrists. He was pale, with fine features and grey hair swept neatly back. But it was his smile that charmed. He smiled with his eyes and it was like a caress. I felt truly welcome as I stammered out "Thank you," and fell silent. He was Alan's boss and his title was inhibiting. I was only used to titled Russians. He turned away leaving me to recover. Lady Evans, white-faced and somehow obviously English, sat next to Alan.

Glancing through the window beside me I was fascinated by clouds sweeping past below us, opening to give fleeting glimpses way down of streets and roofs. Like being on top of Snowdon, I thought. I could see the Empire State Building pointing its tip at the sky, slim and beautiful with its simple lines. I felt light-hearted again, on top of the world. But perspiration was pouring down my back and I had to keep wiping my forehead. As Katia had warned me the heating was overwhelming and my suit hung heavily on me.

I had tucked into a shrimp cocktail, spooning it out to the last tasty bit — we had come from food rationing in Britain — and now enormous juicy steaks were placed before us. Mine was tender and eagerly I wolfed down half. But that was enough. I could not eat another mouthful. However to leave meat on a plate was out of the question. Exchanging glances with Alan we struggled on to the last morsel. I wondered why Sir Francis's lips were twitching. Later we learned that restaurants vie with each other piling up their customers' plates to demonstrate their wealth, wealth signifying success and success being the American

New York

dream.

"My dear," Lady Evans turned to me. "I expect you know that we're leaving in three weeks' time. I'm packing and the farewell ceremonies . . . so forgive me if I don't help you with the bazaar. You will take it over, won't you?"

"Bazaar . . . what bazaar?"

"The Daughters of the British Empire Bazaar. An annual affair. The consulate know all about it. I'm afraid I haven't even time to give you advice. I'm sorry. But you will do it?" She looked tense, a deep furrow between her eyes and dark patches under them.

"Yes, of course." She was so gentle and appealing, I could not refuse her anything. But I was staggered by the news that they were leaving. A new C-G as well as Alan, and we would have to attend all the farewell parties at the same time as settling in ourselves.

Outside the Rainbow Room as I was saying good-bye to the Evanses, Alan thrust an agent's list of houses and flats to rent into my hands.

"Can you start looking straight away? We must find something as soon as possible."

I longed to rest. I felt heavy and sleepy and I seemed to have lived through weeks in just this one morning, but I said, "Yes, of course." The hotel is expensive, I thought, and the children romping around . . .

He hurried on, "Keep to Manhatten, the central part, within easy reach of the office, and on the East side of Fifth Avenue, the West is considered slummy. Look for large, elegant reception rooms. The office car is outside. Take it. Cocktails at six. See you in the hotel at five. Good luck!" He disappeared.

I clutched the list and descended to the crowded, noisy street below. Police cars kept whizzing past, siren blaring. It was a relief to climb into the car. The driver inspected the list and drove to the residential part of Fifth Avenue. The Park was on one side and apartment houses on the other — endless rows of tall, grey blocks of concrete cut by parallel lines of square windows gazing monotonously out. Like one enormous prison, I thought. The car stopped; I jumped out, entered the first block and began the search.

Every apartment looked like a stage-set. Everything was new and spotless with no sign of use. A large woman in a dark gown showed me over the first apartment. Heavy velvet curtains (I imagined Lawrence swinging on them), deep couches, gilt-framed pictures and occasional tables stacked with silver-framed portraits. Everything in place, a set for 'Victoria Regina'.

"I have two children," I told her. The woman looked startled and shook her head.

The next flat looked as though it was prepared for some existentialist play with startling white walls, a wooden couch flush with the floor, covered with white rugs, and chairs of spindly wire lined up against one wall. A young woman in white pyjamas, puffing on a cigarette in a long ebony holder, drawled, "Like it, honey?" Every flat exuded money and all were too expensive. I felt frustrated. The children needed simple furniture while we needed a dignified background. I sighed and drove on from flat to flat.

Suddenly my driver volunteered, "The Temple Emmanuel." The line of cement was broken and I peered up at the giant synagogue, an enormous arched portico under its pediment. I had met an astonishing number of Jewish families in these apartments, most of them speaking Russian. One plump, red-haired matron had called in Russian to someone in another room. "Here comes another . . ."

"I speak Russian," I warned her. Her businesslike manner dropped off her.

"You new here? Like salt cucumbers? Zhe real ones, not pickled?" She ran off and returned with a plateful of salt cucumbers which we munched as we talked.

"You Russian? You need help?" she enquired. I received the same warm welcome in every Jewish apartment. Strange, I thought, these refugees from the notorious Russian pogroms, who have settled and grown rich in the USA, still love things Russian. Their number explained the size of the synagogue. I thought of them as 'foreigners', here in the States; I did not realise that they were as American as anyone else, for all Americans are 'foreigners' except the Red Indians.

My driver announced, 'The Guggenheim Museum'. Massive

concrete walls spiralled up off a concrete platform, like some pre-historic monster dumped from the sky. It was exciting and I laughed as we sped past and into Park Avenue with its long, shining cars — no buses or commercial traffic — gliding between the same square blocks of cement with the same square windows. Inside, luxury flats but all either too expensive, too small or, "Oh, no, no children here." I was tired, hot and discouraged. It was five o'clock and I had found nothing. My feet ached and my head was in a whirl.

Back in the hotel, in the children's room stood six camp beds! Katia, who was reading to Libet on her lap, solved the problem. "You must ask for 'cribs'. These are 'cots'." That was the first of many language misunderstandings.

Mary was bubbling over with excitement. "The drug-store was lovely. We sat on high stools at a long counter and we had double-decker turkey sandwiches and enormous ice-cream sodas."

But Katia, looking embarrassed, drew me aside, "They mustn't go to that drug-store behind the hotel. Your liftmen and doormen eat there. You must go at least several blocks aways." She kissed us all and went off home.

I soaked in a hot bath to recover. Everything was too big, too overwhelming. When I heard Alan return, I shouted, "Nothing so far." I longed to share with him all I had seen, heard and thought. This was our first day in New York, but it was late. We had to hurry. People live so fast here, I don't even have time to think, I grumbled to myself. After quick good-night kisses for the children, we were off.

"Where are we going?" I asked.

Alan, usually placid, burst out, "To the Consul's. He's holding a farewell party for the staff."

"He's leaving too?" I could not believe it.

Frowning, Alan nodded. Even his patience was strained.

"But why change everyone at the same time?"

"It's always happening. They change jobs so rapidly in the Foreign Office, probably no-one quite knows what's going on out here," and he added, "I'll be in charge when Sir Francis leaves until the new C-G arrives." We would be on our own in a new post with a new Consul, Alan working for two, and with no-one to instruct either of us.

"It's infuriating," I exclaimed.

At the party we forgot the F.O. We were the centre of a welcoming, British crowd. Smart girl-secretaries and the so-called locally-engaged staff introduced themselves, asking eagerly, "How are the children? Is the hotel comfortable?"

Then everyone turned smiling towards the door as Sir Francis and Lady Evans entered. Sir Francis toured the room.

"How's the bronchitis? Wife any better?" He knew everyone and from the way he listened I could see he cared.

"He's the most popular boss in the Service," Alan whispered. Lady Evans, settled in an armchair, leant back listening to the chatter. I could see she was worn out. It felt good to be apart of a contented, happy office, but then Sir Francis was leaving . . .

When we came back to the hotel, the children were asleep, but Mary was sobbing. I sympathised but I was yawning my head off as I tucked her up. "Go to sleep, Mary. It'll be all right, dear."

4

Lady Evans' bazaar! It was daunting. I had never organised one before. Back at the Office next morning, I asked for the bazaar file.

"There's no file, Mrs Williams," Mrs Hinkler told me.

"Then where do I get instructions?"

She shrugged.

"You mean someone runs it every year but there are no notes?"

How did they expect me to run an official bazaar, me, a stranger, in a strange place without help or advice? I was appalled but aloud I said, "I'll write everything down as I go along and the office can keep notes."

Mrs Hinkler said nothing but I guessed what her silence meant. Wives were not part of the office; my notes had no place there.

"Well, tell me all you know."

"It's not much, Mrs Williams. The Daughters of the British Empire — D.B.E. they're called — a society of women of British descent — raise money for the Victoria Home for elderly people of British descent. Our Consular commercial section will send out letters, signed by you, to all British firms in New York, asking for donations. That's about it."

It was bigger than I imagined and I'd never dealt with the Commonwealth.

"Better phone the Daughters, Mrs Williams," she added.

The girls in the office knew little more, except that they took turns to sell at the booth.

It had taken the whole morning to find out just this and now I had to hurry back to take Mary and the children to a drug-store further away from the hotel.

The double-decker turkey sandwiches were delicious, I agreed, and it was amusing, perched up on high stools at the counter, watching a fat workman in a brilliant red and green striped shirt, stomach bulging over his belt, who kept shouting "Hi, honey!" at every well-dressed young typist hurrying past, nose in the air. We laughed, he winked at us and I felt reassured.

Once the children were off to the park, I settled down to telephone. I rang the Chairman of the D.B.E. She passed me on to the Vice-Chairman and the Vice-Chairman to another official and then another, till finally the Bazaar Chairman informed me that the 'Faire' was a three-day event to be held in less than a month's time. "Your Commonwealth Booth brings in the bulk of the money," she added, "but as to how it's run, I've no idea. I guess that's up to you, Mrs Williams."

A whole afternoon gone and I was still hovering over the phone when Alan returned. He was frowning. He had his problems too, but I blurted out, "There are no files, no information. I'm supposed to rely on Divine Providence!" He rushed at me, gave me a bear hug that left me gasping, shouted, "Come on. We have to go out," and disappeared into the shower.

"O.K.," I called, laughing. I changed quickly, kissed the children and we were off again.

It was the Consul's farewell party for our Commonwealth colleagues, Canadians, Australians, New Zealanders, South Africans, Indians, and Pakistanis. All these nationalities, the Indians and Pakistanis in colourful saris, greeted each other affectionately, called each other by their first name, laughed and chatted like one big family and crowded round Sir Francis, who was clearly a favourite. It was heart-warming but my head was full of too many new impressions and worries about the apartment, the children and the bazaar. I could not take in any more new faces or impressions and I was emotionally drained. I needed calm to digest it all. Racing from event to event left me dazed. I sipped my whisky and longed for bed.

Next morning I heard retching and running water next door. I jumped out of bed. The children lay in their cots, pale-faced, their foreheads wet. Mary stood between them, red-eyed and her face one big yawn. "I'm dead tired, Mrs Williams. They've been sick all night."

"Oh Mary! I have to look at two flats first, but then I'll take over. Just carry on for a little bit longer." It's the change of climate, the over-heated rooms and I wondered what was added to the food we were eating. I had neglected the children. They clung to Mary, the only stable element in this unfamiliar life, but she was out of her depth too.

I dressed quickly and hurried out. The flats were small, dark, and unsuitable for entertaining. I had just returned when Mamoo caught me,

"Please, Masha darling. Get me an electric hot-plate. It's the food that disagrees with the children. They need some good nourishing chicken broth with vegetables." She was carrying a heavy shopping basket. She had already bought the food.

I called, "Back in a jiffy Mary," and rushed out again. Bloomingdale's was not far, I had heard. A bus, and I was there. I bought the electric hot-plate and returned in no time, dashing now at the speed of a true New Yorker. I just had to get the phone numbers of the Commonwealth C-Gs' wives from the office, which they had promised to have ready, and at last I was able to send Mary off to sleep.

I wiped the children's faces and ran back and forth to the bathroom, emptying basins. Then I read the children's favourite, Squirrel Nutkin.

"This is a Tale about a Tail . . ." They smiled, giggled and soon joined in, 'Riddle me, riddle me, rot-tot-tote!' Meanwhile delicious smells of chicken broth spread through the rooms.

At five I had to wake Mary; we had to go out.

"All right dear?" She yawned and rubbed her eyes.

"Yes, I'll manage." I plunged into a bath to wash away the sickroom smell.

Though the Evans' farewell parties were in full swing, Alan and I had to attend a reception for the opening of the International Horse Show. It was a white tie affair at the Waldorf Astoria, New York's most famous hotel. Just as we were ready to go Mamoo rushed into the flat eyes wide, wisps of hair over her face, her jacket askew.

"I've been robbed," she blurted out. "A youth darted out from behind a car." Every evening she insisted on walking back to

Katia's in the dark but through a peaceful, residential district or so we had thought.

"Darling, are you hurt?" I put my arm round her.

"No, no. Though he knocked me down against the railings and snatched my bag." Alan drew up an armchair and we sat her down.

"I shouted, 'Thief! Catch him!' but, my dears, the doormen did not move. So inconsiderate of them and no-one in Madison Avenue paid any attention, though I chased the youth. Then I lost sight of him. My glasses, my address book and more sadly the key to Katia's flat are gone."

"I must get you some hot, sweet tea," I interrupted.

"But children, I'm all right. You don't have to fuss".

"And a rug," Alan started for the bedroom.

But poor Katiousha! She'll have to change the keys to her apartment."

We asked for sheets and blankets and arranged a bed for Mamoo on the couch.

We set off once more for the Waldorf Astoria. I squeezed Alan's arm as I swept into the banqueting hall, head up, in my most beautiful evening gown, a made-to-measure black velvet, that fitted closely with a tight bodice, narrow shoulder straps and a very full skirt. Under the huge crystal chandeliers the men's black clothes set off the women's richly decorated gowns and glittering jewels; their faces looked almost natural in the artificial light. Alan kept peering at their low décolletages; I caught his arm and cried, "Look!" pointing away at the candles on the round tables sparkling over the silver, the white damask tablecloths and rigid napkins.

The national flags flew over each competing nation's table. We found the Union Jack above a notice 'England', and joined the British team. Col. Llewellyn, our captain, a black-haired, slim, elegant figure, was grumbling. "England indeed! White here comes from Wales, like me. In fact, we're all Welshmen this year. Why can't they get things right?"

Advocado pears stuffed with crab meat distracted him and he chatted with Alan about that afternoon's loss when White took a wrong jump. I concentrated on the food. I knew nothing about show jumping but Alan as usual held his own. I must learn to do that too. I must learn to be more positive, I thought.

Each captain made a speech. When it was Col. Llewelyn's turn, he rose and with all eyes on him, he jabbed a finger at the caption 'England' and shouted, "We're not an English team. We're a British team . . ." Alan tugged at his jacket and whispered, "Forget it. Tell them later," but Llewelyn went on, "We're Welshmen. You can call us 'British' but get it right for Pete's sake . . ." We were embarrassed, but guests smiled up at him and clapped enthusiastically when he sat down, still muttering.

Over coffee people moved around. Alan and the team disappeared to greet friends. Presumably Alan thought that just as he went off to 'do his stuff' as he called socialising, so I would get on with 'my stuff'. In any case he never minded sitting or standing on his own. He found it a relief. I looked round. I did not know anyone. Those at nearby tables stared at me. I tried to drink my coffee nonchalantly. I must feel natural, but with the Union Jack before me, I was not myself. It wasn't me they were staring at. I was Great Britain. I felt acutely self-conscious. Sir Francis in public appeared natural, so did Alan. Must be the result of years of training.

A young man, face bright red, forehead glistening, lurched towards me. "All alone, honey?" He grasped the edge of the table and leaned across, wafting alcohol fumes. I shrank from him. He was repulsive and I wasn't used to drunks. I felt helpless.

"Hi, Stan!" A friend greeted him.

"Hiya!" the young man turned and clutching the friend's shoulder, staggered off. I looked round nervously. I had to sit there till Alan returned. I sipped coffee and iced water and chain-smoked, hoping no-one else would approach. I did not dare look up as this might attract another drunk. I started yawning. I was so tired and soon I had to clench my teeth and pretend to blow my nose.

When Alan had come back at last, as we left, in the hotel corridor, an old lady, her décolletage indecently low, and festooned with jewelry, tottered along, steadying herself with her hands against the wall. I stopped,

"What's she doing? Is she ill? Should we help her?"

Alan laughed, "She's drunk." Now I noticed her glazed eyes.

At a lunch party a few days later, our hostess asked her neighbour at table, "When did you come out?"

"Last week. And you? I sure didn't think you'd be out that soon."

"I've been out several weeks."

Mystified, I asked Alan later, "Where are they coming out from? Surely not prison?"

He grinned. "No. Clinics for alcoholics." In New York society, I learnt, drunks were not the exception and no-one worried about loss of dignity.

Outside we climbed into the car and I flopped on to the back seat. It was the beginning to get light. We've been in New York three days, I thought, and it feels like years. I closed my eyes.

"Darling!" I murmured.

"Um?"

"You need three wives. One for the family, one for the social stuff and one for that bazaar." My head fell on his shoulder and I slept.

5

Flat-hunting, the bazaar, the Evans' farewell parties all clashed and crowded in on us at one and the same time.

First flat-hunting. I lowered my sights and concentrated on flats within our price limit. In the first one I visited, the owner switched on the light. I stood in a large drawing room, pink lampshades shed a warm glow over deep arm-chairs and couches — an elegant apartment, but this was morning! Outside was a bright, crisp, sunny day. I looked out of the window across a narrow street and stared straight at a family sitting down to a meal in the flat opposite. I looked up — nothing but lighted windows and dirty, grey concrete, no glimpse of sky. To live all day in artificial light, no! And boxed into such a cage!

"No, I'm afraid it's not suitable," I said and hurried home. Every morning now I rushed from flat to flat. All equally dark. I began to despair and, as I grumbled "nothing so far," to Alan, I had a guilty feeling that perhaps we should take what was available. There might not be flats with daylight at our price.

But I also had to get those donations for the bazaar from the Commonwealth C-Gs' wives. I phoned round, inviting them to tea.

Canada: "I can only do Tuesday."

New Zealand: "Not Tuesday. Only Monday."

India: "Must ask husband."

South Africa had a bad cold.

The Australian C-G: "There's no C-G's wife."

"Why not?"

"General Smart is not married."

"Sorry. I didn't know (But I should have known, I thought). Who is his deputy?"

Pakistan could come any time.

I phoned back and forth. India was still vague, "Husband say he not know. Will ask Secretary." The others began saying, "Mrs Williams, I'm a busy woman . . ." I apologised. These ladies were senior to me. I was only a Deputy's wife.

"I'm terribly sorry," I kept repeating as I rang back again and again. Finally an afternoon was fixed. The ladies arrived, India in a glamorous blue silk sari, Pakistan very much the New Yorker in a dark suit and vivid make-up. They all agreed to ask for donations till I reached Pakinstan.

"Mrs Shakri, will you collect the Pakistani donations?"

"Sorry, honey. No way. I can't do that."

"As wife of the Pakistani C-G?"

"What's that?"

I swallowed. "Aren't you Mrs Shakri?"

"Sure."

"And you live in the Plaza Hotel?"

"Sure, but I'm American. I have nothing to do with Pakistan."

India bust out laughing, swaying back and forth. "What coincidence! Same name, same hotel!"

"I'm sorry," I sounded like a gramaphone record. "It's a mistake. This is a meeting of the Commonwealth Consul-Generals' wives." I got up to see her out.

"But I'd sure like to help," and she sat on. I fetched her coat. She laid it behind her. I remained standing. She chatted on. I perched on the arm of my chair. She would not go. The others were smiling as they drank their tea. Then they left, Mrs Shakri saying, "Be sure to let me know when you're meeting next. I'll make a point of being there." Impossible to fix another date in her presence. All that phoning to do again.

At the same time the farewell parties for the Evanses were in full flow and protocol demanded that as their Deputies we should accompany them.

Mrs Kermit Roosevelt, the widow of a son of Theodore Roosevelt, gave a buffet supper. At the door of her brown-stone house, Sir Francis told us, "She was a great friend of Franklin D. Politically they were on opposite sides, but she's a great lady, tolerant, kind and pro-British. You'll like her." Alan gave me a reassuring nod as we followed the Evanses into a smoke-filled room, full of men in dark suits and women in dark dresses with strings of pearls. That year's fashion made a lugubrious spectacle. The noise was deafening and it was some time before I could distinguish words.

Mrs Roosevelt, a slim, smiling woman, shook us warmly by the hand and then Alan and I slipped away, leaving her free to concentrate on the Evanses, her guests of honour.

Alan muttered, "I must do my stuff," and disappeared into the crowd. I knew that he had to mix, gather local opinion and put across the British point of view, and, I supposed, I ought to do the same. I knew no-one but Americans introduce themselves, a helpful habit.

"I'm Ted Jackson. I'm a lawyer," a guest approached me. I couldn't have taken him for an Englishman with that well-scrubbed look as if he had just emerged from a hot bath, collar and cuffs a startling white, a crew cut and rimless glasses that made him look severe though he smiled easily. We shook hands. I was too self-conscious to introduce myself and murmoured our traditional, meaningless "How do you do?"

He exclaimed, "What a tragedy that you English have a Labour government."

"Why a tragedy?"

"Your socialism is just another kind of Russian communism. Everything under government control."

I laughed, "It isn't at all."

"Of course it is. Look at your National Health Service."

"But I'm proud of it. It's a wonderful achievement. No-one need fear ill health for financial reasons."

He shrugged. "What you need is our competitive private enterprise system. You're nationalised, finished." I was to hear that same argument time and time again. We were to mix mostly with moneyed people, Republicans, and I soon realised that private enterprise dominated their thinking and 'liberalism' was a dirty word. But it was a relief that at social gatherings Americans discuss topics that matter and not, as so often in Britain, only polite nothings, the three most interesting subjects — politics, religion and work — being taboo. Here I would never be bored.

I found myself beside a tall, thin young man with thick glasses. He was, it appeared, a teacher from the Middle West.

"What do you teach?" I asked.

At first he was silent. Then he blurted out, "I'm not teaching at the moment," and he stared down at the floor.

"Oh?" I queried.

He inhaled deeply on his cigarette, letting the smoke emerge through his nostrils. He was so very serious and unsmiling.

"I guess I might as well confess. I've lost my job. I'm accused of being a communist." I waited. "You want to know why?" I nodded. "I attended a lecture by your Harold Lasky. That's all they have against me." He downed his whisky. I watched in silence. "You've heard of Senator McCarthy?" I nodded again. I knew McCarthy was leading a witch-hunt and had accused the most improbable people, even Dean Acheson, the Secretary of State for Foreign Affairs, of communist affiliation. Acheson had stated publicly that 'Communism is fatal to independent governments and to free people,' but he became suspect for also stating that 'We are not attempting to change the government or social structure of the Soviet Union.'

In London before we came to the USA, Alan once told me we had to inform the Foreign Office before gong to a party given by a friend's son.

"But why?" I had asked.

"He's a communist."

"So what?"

"That's the rule these days. Foreign Service Officers are not supposed to associate with communists without permission." I thought that ridiculous, but this was sheer nonsense. I noticed the young man's hands were not quite steady.

"Belle Roosevelt is a loyal, exceptional friend," he went on. Evidently his other friends avoided him. He kept his voice low. He was frightened even here in this house, I realised. It's monstrous, I thought, and how is it that one Senator can have so much power? I had thought the USA was a haven for the persecuted, a champion of tolerance. I could not ask or express sympathy. Alan had drummed into me that we must never discuss American policy, never even appear to meddle in America's internal affairs. I stared at the young anxious face and I longed to help, to do something.

"Well, let's have another drink," I suggested. He grinned and went off with our empty glasses.

Back home, I told Alan. "It's incredible. He lost his job just for attending a lecture!"

"I know. It's tragic."

The Evanses had been in New York seven years. Societies as well as private people wished to give them a grand send-off, and we followed them around like a Lord and Lady-in-Waiting. Sir Francis kept smiling at me. "Bearing up? It won't be long now."

At cocktail parties Sir Francis' neat, grey head and Lady Evans' black velvet beret were only just visible at the centre of a jostling crowd.

At banquets Sir Francis sat on the dais flanked by officials, with Lady Evans, in a sleeveless, yellow chiffon dress, smiling shyly, sipping iced water and hardly touching her food, her mind presumably on the chaos back home, packing cases, trunks, clothes strewn about, a seven-year accumulation of knick-knacks to be packed.

Alan and I, sitting with other guests below, listened to speech after speech. When Sir Francis leant over the table, delicate fingers resting on it, his fine-featured face so distinguished, I thought he was an honour to Britain. He spoke without notes and looked down on the audience with so much affection as though saying, 'So many friends down there!'

When the British Societies honoured him, the faces staring up at the dais were serious, unusual in the States where, I had noticed, everyone was expected to grin, whatever the occasion. They must be worried, I thought. Sir Francis was speaking.

"For Britain to survive it is imperative that you increase your exports . . ." To survive! But we had won the war, we were still the greatest nation. "We must strengthen the Commonwealth . . ." Commonwealth — no longer Empire. I sat there as tense as those around me. Certainly there was rationing at home. Britain was exhausted after the war effort, but other countries were in the same state. However I could not ignore the anxiety on the faces round me. Americans, I had learnt, have no time for weakness; they only admire success and they are suspicious of our Labour government. I sat twirling my wine glass round and round. "But we have the brains, the know-how; we will succeed." Yes, we would. I was determined. I'd do my bit. I refused . . . I hesitated even to consider it . . . to sink into insignificance.

When addressing American audiences, I realised Sir Francis was making a tremendous effort to use this last opportunity to rekindle faith in Britain's future, to stress the importance of preserving the links established during the war. I considered Americans immature, their country an ex-colony, not up to our standards, but Sir Francis addressed them as equals. I've so much to learn, I realised.

"Britain and America," Sir Francis smiled, "are experiencing the antagonism, love, irritation and frustration of a father and son. But the son impulsive, longing to use his muscle, still needs the experience, wisdom and restraining hand of his old father," and Sir Francis stroked his grey hairs. The audience laughed and applauded. He concluded, "I love this country, this beloved son, and I am not ashamed to proclaim it."

The audience rose to their feet, clapped and burst into 'For He's a Jolly Good Fellow'. I was filled with affection for these lovable Americans and I was almost moved to tears, carried away as usual by emotion, but then I saw Alan grinning at me. Sir Francis sat down and smiled across at Lady Evans. She was clapping too, standing up but she was leaning against the table and I guessed she needed that support. The guests left chatting, joking, their confidence restored.

One day was exceptionally wearing for the Evanses with the Installation of the new Bishop of New York, an exhausting two-hour ceremony and an Ulster Irish farewell meeting. That night we met up again for a five-course dinner in their honour at Mr Green's, the Canadian C-G; I was very tired and I could imagine how the Evanses felt.

When the champagne was finally brought in, Mr Green heaved himself up like a big, heavy bear, and began, "Sir Francis and Lady Evans! Frank and Mary! We all want to wish you the best of luck . . ."

Suddenly Lady Evans remarked quietly, "I can't take any more," and burst into tears. Covering her face with a handkerchief, she rose and hurried out of room. The guests stared speechless after her, Mr Green still standing, mouth open. I wanted to follow her but I hardly knew her. I hesitated, then sat on embarrased, like everyone else.

"She's tired . . . all that packing . . ." Sir Francis murmoured and we all began talking, but I thought, how humiliating for her and it might well happen to me!

As we drove home Alan remarked, "It shows what a strain they're under. She's such a matter-of-fact person." I sighed. They could not refuse invitations. Their hosts would not understand and the good-will they had built up would be lost.

"I should have gone to her," I cried, "I should have helped her. That's what I'm here for. Oh, I wish I had not let her down." Alan pressed my hand.

6

I found the perfect flat. In a spacious drawing-room broad windows gave on to Central Park, sunlight streamed on to elegant, antique furniture, upholstered in a rich, dark red, and on to a patterned Turkish carpet — a beautiful room, made for entertaining. A library, light and cheerful, with shelves up to the ceiling crammed with tempting books, deep couches and arm-chairs, protected by brightly-coloured washable loose covers; we could sink into them, put our feet up and the children's sticky fingers could do no damage. As it was a corner flat, light poured into the three large bedrooms with bathrooms attached.

The flat was on the fourth floor of a building on Fifth Avenue at 98th Street, rather close to Harlem, exclusively negro, and dangerous to enter, or so we had been told (extraordinary to find a dangerous ghetto in the opulent States), but there was less traffic and cleaner air. This was what I had been searching for. I took a deep, thankful breath of relief.

There was ample space in the kitchen and pantry and the dining-room could seat twenty. I imagined us bent over chocolate soufflés in décolleté evening dress, candle-light playing over our sparkling jewels. I laughed and stepped beyond it to look for the maids' quarters where there should be room for Mamoo.

Complete darkness! I drew back and switched on the light. Two tiny grey cells, the length of a bed and half its length in width, with sitting-up bath tubs in niches alongside. Narrow, grimly windows stared into a court-yard, from whose murky depth rose the screeching and throbbing of machinery and the clatter of dust-bins. No daylight and this was supposed to be 'home' for two women! How could Mamoo live here?

I hurried back to the hotel, but Mamoo assured me, "I know the kind of rooms but with the door open between them, I shall have adequate space. I only need to sleep there. The room at

Katia's is no better." Mamoo was indifferent to her surroundings. She existed only for her beloved families. We teased her that she was almost as family-minded as another Russian mother, who, we maintained, prayed daily, 'Oh God, take everything from everyone and give it to my children.'

The rent was 425 dollars a month. Alan would have to fight for an increase in our rent allowance but as he said, "I've done that at every post so far and the Consulate will back me." They did and the flat was ours. At last that problem solved.

We had drinks with the owners. In the entrance hall hung a life-sized portrait of George Washington.

"You don't object?" the owner asked.

"Not at all," Alan assured him. "He's the first Englishman to make good in America." They laughed.

We could move in three weeks' time, just before the bazaar. The move and the bazaar so close together, I thought, but it could not be helped. And I was progressing with the bazaar. In between lunches and cocktails I rushed to Alan's office and appropriated his telephone. The right Mrs Shakri promised to collect Pakistani donations and the girls in the office now volunteered bits of information ... someone sat at the cash register ... Commonwealth girls did shifts ... Commonwealth flags were displayed ... and Crests ... a trip to Bermuda was raffled. I was advancing.

One evening Alan came home exclaiming, "We have the evening off!" At last we could rest and go early to bed!

"But it's Katia's party," Mamoo protested. "My dears, if you're free, please go." She looked distressed.

Alan sighed. "Must we really?"

"Yes. Yes. You haven't met all the family yet. Please, Alan! They'll be disappointed." Yes, they would. They knew nothing of the life we led. They would not understand. Were we not living in luxury? Alan looked at me and reluctantly I nodded.

I knew the kind of guests Katia would invite. She had always craved for elegance in dress, in surroundings, and in manners. We were born into the highest Russian society, but Alan's parents were committed Fabians and I was apprehensive.

Kapa Nebolsine, Katia's husband, opened the door shouting, "Come in! Come in!" He kissed my hand and I, his forehead.

"Hullo Alan!" They shook hands. Kapa stood shorter than Alan. Handsome with a neat head and a side parting, he wore a beautifully-cut suit. Kapa had made money, a rare achievement for a Russian refugee. He ran his own hydraulic engineering business. Russian friends, potential Oblomovs, shook their heads as he flew around the world seeking out contracts. "Must be his English mother," they told themselves.

Kapa waved his arms in welcome, calling "Katia! Come here. Here's Alan."

My sister look very distinguished in her plain, black silk dress and double row of heavy pearls. Though their flat was surprisingly small and dark, the drawing-room was as elegant as Katia herself. Antique upright settees and chairs, their seats embroidered in petit-point, were pushed back against the walls. Soft lighting glowed on the golden halos of the Virgin and Child on the ikon hanging in the corner. It lit up the gilded frames round the portraits of the late Russian Emperor and his family on the wall. There were engravings of St. Petersburg and Moscow.

The room was crowded, the noise deafening. Guests gestured extravagantly. Men bowed and kissed the ladies' hands. The ladies kissed, their arms r̈und each other. Katia introduced Alan to Princes, Princesses, Counts and Countesses and she left him talking to a young woman. The rounded curves of her face, the high cheek bones and wide-spaced, slanting eyes gave her a kindly, cheeful look; her hair lay in natural waves and her high colour was her own — a typical Russian, I thought and was relieved to see Alan beaming at her.

There was something puzzling about her and the other women present. Though they spoke with American accents, they did not fit into my idea of American women. Then I realised — they were just themselves, without the artificial social manner that western women automatically adopt. They did not adjust their faces and postures to circumstances; they looked you straight in the face and their laughter was spontaneous.

Around Alan and with their eye on him, friends were asking, "How's Verochka?"

"Fine. Fine."

"How's Sonechka and Lisenka?" Always the diminutive. I laughed to myself. Among these Russian aristocrats it was Alan with his working-class background who was the VIP.

Friends of my childhood hurried up, "Hullo Masha! Haven't seen you in a long time," Vera cried, a handsome, slim woman in whom I immediately recognised the little girl with two plaits with whom I had tried to ride a scooter and we fell laughing so many times. We smiled and kissed. Then she asked, "Seen the Petrovs?"

"No."

"Have you been to the Orloffs?"

"No." She looked at me strangely. These families formed the centre of Russian community life.

"We mix with Americans," I explained.

"Oh, Americans ..." and she fell silent. Some Russians had married Americans, there was no-one else to marry, but they tried to Russianise them.

"How long have you been here?" I asked.

"Four years. We came from Germany. My husband was a volunteer interpreter with the German armed forces on the Russian front." So he had helped the Germans against his own people. But I remembered that here Soviet Russians were considered Bolsheviks, murderers, barbarians who should be exterminated. My compatriots here had never met Soviets face to face as I had, had not worked among them as I had nor had they heard their point of view. They continued spreading all the old hatreds whereas for me that was all past. And at the same time I realised that they were trying to preserve their former Russianness, whereas I was acquiring Britishness.

I fell silent. We had shared too many childhood secrets to be casual acquaintances now yet we were too far apart to be friends. I didn't know how to rise above these differences and how to bridge the gulf between us. I simply condemned her and her like.

She nodded and turned away.

Kapa was balancing a plateful of 'zakusky' (hors d'oeuvres) in one hand and bottle of vodka in the other.

"I prepared these myself," he boasted. "Alan, a glass of vodka.

Nadia – my sister-in-law

Drink it bottoms up and you'll avoid a headache. A bit of salt herring?"

Everyone spoke in English — an astonishing achievement on Katia's part. Russians normally congregate in corners and whisper in Russian even when their hosts do not understand.

"Hi, Alan!" My second sister, Natasha, had driven up from Maryland where she lived with her husband and two children. Alan gazed into her enormous bright blue eyes with their long curly lashes. In a white blouse with a frilly collar, over a dark skirt, she was slim and very feminine. She was carrying a tray with meat balls in sour cream and mixed salads. Alan leant across it and kissed her eagerly, but I was not jealous. When we were girls, Natasha had carried off the few boy-friends I had. She played with young men like a cat with mice. She was lively and never took them seriously. I cared and became stiff and awkward. Now secure in my marriage, I was amused as I watched her fluttering her eyelashes at Alan.

"I have to help Katia," she smiled and her mouth twisted sideways, showing perfect, white teeth. Then she disappeared, passing Alan on to a distant relative, a professor who peered through thick lenses and lisped into his face.

As we drove away, Alan murmoured, "That was very pleasant. They're so natural. I'm glad we came." High praise from a normally monosyllabic husband. I squeezed his arm.

Next Saturday we were free again.

"Let's go to Vania's, in the country," I begged.

Alan agreed, "Might as well do the whole family and get it over with."

Vania fetched us from the hotel in his car. His wife, Nadia, a small, plump figure with a lively face and black eyes darting here and there appraising us, sprang out of the car and hugged and kissed me.

We swept smoothly out of New York's concrete dust and dirt, across the Triborough Bridge, spanning the East River, and along the Parkway, into a restful scene of broad, tree-lined lanes and white wooden houses, surrounded by unfenced gardens. Nadia chatted

"You look just as I expected."

"And so do you!" I exclaimed.

Vania broke in, "We're nearly in Sea Cliff. It's a township on Long Island Sound. We have a big Russian colony here and I'm responsible for it to the State Department. There's always someone in trouble, usually over immigration documents. Some refugees never learn English. We hold open house at week-ends."

Their three-storied white, wooden houses was crammed with Russians. At least twenty were seated at a long table covered with a white cloth. Vania presided, his large bulk dominating the company. Mrs. Wadkovsky, Nadia's mother, a wiry lady, kept placing huge, square pies, some with carrots, some with minced meat and cabbage, before him. With slow, deliberate movements, Vania sliced off large portions.

"Kushaite! Kushaite!" (Eat! Eat!) Mrs Wadkovsky's shrill voice rose above the hubbub.

"Po Anglishky, Mama," Nadia whispered (In English, Mama).

More guests poured in and there were cries of, "Hullo, Maria Evgenevna!"

"How are you, Petr Petrovich?"

"And you Ivan Vasilievich?"

Alan whispered, "These names . . . ?"

"Patronyms. Ivan, son of Vasili. There are no Mr or Mrs in Russian."

New arrivals squeezed in at the table, as others left. Move plates were provided, more pies, fruit, cheese. In the midst of it all Alan sat bemused beside a silent man with a long face and deep-set eyes — a face from an ikon.

"That's Vasia, Nadia's brother and Natasha's former husband," I whispered. Brother and sister had married brother and sister. But Natasha was now divorced and re-married. Alan shook his head; he was beyond taking in more relatives.

Coming back on the double-decker train, I asked Alan, "Well?"

He laughed. "All these relations! It's been a powerful shock, but I still live." And what a pleasant respite from official life, I thought.

7

We were home in the new flat and now, I thought, we can relax, settle into a routine and have some peace. We explored our sun-lit rooms and the children dug into the crates.

"My cups! My little dollies!" Libet exclaimed, and "Look! Look, my got!" Lawrence shouted. Dolls, teddy bears, trucks littered the nursery floor. In her room Mary fixed a Crucifix and a gaudy postcard of the Virgin above her bed. Mamoo, now mistress of the kitchen, her ample figure covered by a blue and white striped apron, unpacked huge cartons bursting with avocado pears, courgettes and other delicious vegetables and fruit. Alan, in a pair of old grey flannels, sat perched up a ladder counting rose-patterned plates, cups and saucers while I squatted below, ticking figures off the inventory. As we worked through the morning and afternoon, Mamoo plied us with coffee and chicken sand-wiches. Fill the stomach and they'll be healthy and happy, was her belief. At last our life seemed normal.

I got up. "I must see if Mary has found the playground in the park. I told her to stay there with the children." We were an out-of-door family and the park drew us like a magnet. But Katia had insisted that, "Central Park is dangerous. If Alan isn't with you, you must stay on the path at the edge or inside the playground."

I was incredulous. The park in the middle of New York dangerous! So I had checked with a local official at a dinner party and he explained, "Immigrants to the States pour into New York. When they find jobs, they disperse throughout the country, but the dregs, the sick, the drug addicts, they stay here and haunt the park."

I hurried out. Mary was sitting on a bench, smiling up at a young policeman astride a chestnut horse. He was laughing down at her, his back stiff in the dark, blue uniform with the double row of brass buttons. Behind her Lawrence was jumping from outgrowths of rock, while Libet stood very still under a tree as a squirrel squatted in front of her, its paws on her hand nibbling a biscuit on her palm.

As I came up Mary blushed down her face and neck. She had such a fair skin. The policeman touched his cap. "I was telling her, Mam, that it ain't safe here. She gotta stay in the playground. And these bushes ... The children gotta stay away from them. She mustn't let the children out of her sight."

Mary jumped up, gave him a quick look, called the children and together we went through the gap in the high wire fence surrounding the playground. Such a wealthy city, I thought, and people cage their children for protection.

Inside children swarmed over chutes, swings, see-saws and sand-pits and raised the dust as they rushed past. They screamed at each other, "That's mine!" "Get off!" and their mothers screamed at them, "Don't honey!" "Stop it, baby!" Mary and I settled on a bench. Lawrence was already careering down a chute and Libet was making a bed for her dolly in a sand-pit.

"It's horrid here," Mary complained, and so lovely among the trees and rocks." I agreed but refrained from commenting on the handsome companion out there.

Mary kept glancing at me.

"What is it, Mary?"

"Could I? I mean ... I've been invited to the Donegal Club dance." Mary came from Donegal. "There's another nanny going; I met her just now and she'll fetch and see me home."

"That's all right then but stay together." Mary, so attractive and gentle, will soon make friends, I thought, and the nightly sobbing will cease. Women kept stopping and staring at our children and Mary explained, "People keep asking where we come from and why we have rosy cheeks. The children here are pasty-faced. They even admire Lawrence." She was referring to the rash Lawrence still had on his face and neck. I was to take him to the doctor next morning.

I sat there and relaxed. The children now have their play-ground, Mary is making friends, Mamoo has her cooking and Alan and I have a home. New York had just been hectic and difficult at first.

Next morning a sudden fierce wind roared round the block. In the park branches swayed and creaked. The wind whirled round us clutching at our clothes as Lawrence and I waited outside on our way to the doctor. The doorman was fetching a taxi. Suddenly a violent gust hit us, lifted Lawrence into the air and, before I could move, hurled him into the street, right in front of the approaching taxi. I lunged forward, grabbed at him and just managed to haul him back as the breaking taxi brushed our clothes. The taximan gasped, "Sorry, Mam, sorry. I couldn't stop that quick!" I was trembling as we climbed in.

"Tail-end of a hurricane," the doorman shouted. But Lawrence grinned as I held him tightly.

The doctor pronounced his a 'wonderful specimen' and prescribed a strict diet with no milk as it was 'homogenised' and 'enriched' and he wasn't used to it. We drove back safely but there was no going out again. The children were happy enough indoors; Lawrence sat on the kitchen table, dangling his legs while Mamoo prepared special dishes for her beloved boy. Libet was cuddled up on Mary's lap in the nursery where they were reading 'Little Black Sambo.'

But I was desperate. The bazaar! All the last minute jobs to do and here I was stranded. I must keep calm. Better make a list of what still needs doing. I sat down by the window.

Stick price labels on goods.

Distribute duty rotas to Commonwealth Consulates.

Outside tiles hurtled down the street, bits of scaffolding crashed to the ground. Pedestrians rubbed dirt and dust from their eyes as it swirled across the streets. Worried, I turned on the radio. The music was interrupted and I caught the words '. . . present storm emergency situation . . . winds of eighty miles per hour.' In the park, trees leant dangerously sideways. Suddenly a heavy branch split off its trunk, hovered in mid-air and, as I held my breath, crashed to the ground. Alan! He must be on his way home. He will have dismissed the staff. And all this just as I was thinking we could settle down to peace and calm. I felt battered and buffeted by events like the trees in the storm outside. I forced myself back to my list.

Remind India to produce a flag.

Get South African Crest.

The music stopped again. 'Firemen, welfare officers and civil defence personnel are all alerted.' I sat rigid. Then the Mayor came on, "I am speaking to all the citizens of New York. Stay at home under shelter." Why isn't Alan home? I clutched the pencil in my hand, my list forgotten. "Folks keep away from the park. People have been crushed by falling trees." Why wasn't Alan here? That slender Empire State Building unprotected, alone up in the sky. Oh God! I got up, gripped the window-sill, stared down at the empty street. I mustn't panic. But it was always this way. On our honeymoon climbing a mountain I had dropped behind. Up above I saw a man, a rifle over his shoulder. He was approaching Alan, he was about to shoot him! I clambered up, sweating, heart pounding. The man passed Alan, and then me. He gave me a quick, strange glance.

"Oh Alan, thank God!" I panted.

"Why? What's the matter?"

"I thought he was going to shoot you!" Alan stared at me just as the man had done, "Why on earth?" I said nothing, but I clutched his arm. Alan teased and laughed all the way home. Now, when he said, 'Oh, do stop fussing', which was often, he added, 'No-one's going to shoot me.' This fear for him. It was unreasonable, but I could not control it. Another time I had shouted up to him, "Keep back from that precipice!" When I reached him, he was standing, eyebrows raised, on the edge of a grassy incline sloping gently down. Oh Alan, if anything should happen to him . . .

I heard the key turn in the lock. He was safe! I ran into the hall. He's not going to know I panicked, I decided. But as he stood there, solid, alive, I was unable, as usual, to keep anything from him.

"Oh Alan you're safe. I was so frightened." I gasped and clung to him.

He laughed and kissed me. "Silly! I'm O.K. Actually it was exciting." His cheeks were puce and his hair ruffled up. "The noise in the office was terrific; couldn't hear myself write. We sent the staff home. Then our interior partition walls started cracking." I held tightly on to him. "Part of the ceiling crashed down on to my desk. So I pushed off too. Coming down the lift kept banging against the sides of the shafts. It wasn't exactly pleasant." Thank God I had not known.

Next morning on the breakfast table, on the front page of the Herald Tribune, was a huge face of a dead man, the top of his head smashed in, blood trickling down into his gasping mouth. He was framed in a railway carriage window. I felt sick and for a long time I kept seeing that face. Why shock us, I wondered, when there is nothing we can do to help?

"There's been a bad smash on the Long Island Railway. Seventy seven people killed," Alan said. Inside the paper we were faced with whole pages of photographs of the wounded being treated in hospital. One page showed what looked like a mummy, a tube protruding from the bandaged folds where the mouth should be; I crushed the paper and thrust it quickly into the dust-bin. The others must not see it.

"I should have expected the doctors to stop these stunts," Alan declared. "The people must be suffering from shock." Then he added, "But it seems to be accepted here."

But like any other sensation-seeking New Yorkers, before rushing off to the office, we hurried into the park to view the heavy trunks of trees sprawling over the ground. As I gazed down at them, I realised, there can never be peace and calm in New York. It isn't that kind of city. Ah well, and anyway the bazaar was upon me.

8

The bazaar! Planks, trestles, packing cases littered the Biltmore Hotel ballroom as workmen trundled in more piles of cases. 'Daughters of the British Empire' tripped around on high heels, protesting above the general hubbub, "Honey, not here!" and "No, this is our corner!" Dorrie Thomas and I stood in the midst of it all, in the central space alotted to our Commonwealth Booth. Dorrie, plump and smiling, was the new Consul's wife. She had only arrived the day before.

I gazed round nervously. Crates of goods were piles up around us but the trestle tables were not yet set up though the bazaar was to open next day. What was I supposed to do?

"Get a handyman, girls," the President of the Daughters, tall, with red curls piled up on her head, called as she sped past.

I stepped up to a workman with tools protruding from his boiler suit, "Please . . ." He brushed past me. Another appeared, "Please would you . . ."

"Sorry, busy . . ."

I plucked up courage and grabbed the next man's arm. "Put our trestle tables up, please. We can't lay out the goods without them.

"Lady, I gotta finish the stage first." But I clung to him, "No, no. Our stall first." He grinned and shouted to a pal, "Here Jo, give us a hand."

The four tables formed a square with bars above from which to hang more goods. Dorrie and I exchanged smiles. The first hurdle was overcome. I had an idea.

"Let's lay the flags out and display the goods on them. They're so colourful." We spread the Star Spangled Banner over the table first — a gesture of courtesy since most Daughters were now American citizens.

"You can't do that!" I started. A Daughter glared at us,

pointing a finger at the flag. "You can't cover our American flag with goods!"

"No. No. Certainly not!" Others gathered round. I flushed and quickly removed the flag, murmuring, "I'm sorry. I didn't realise."

"Disrespectful! Whatever next!" they exclaimed as they returned to their stalls. Dorrie and I exchanged glances and looked away. We must not laugh.

"We'll hang the flags at the corners and from the bar," I decided. They were four foot long, except India's which was a miniature table-flag in a stand. We fixed the Union Jack at the front in the centre and stood the Indian flag below it.

Next we turned to the crates. Dorrie looked older than me, probably in her mid-forties, but her short figure shot up and down like a Jack-in-the-Box, lifting, unwrapping, placing items on the table and diving back in again. My back ached and I leant against the table.

Dorrie smiled, "I'll take the things out and you arrange them on the table." What a treasure, I thought, as I nodded gratefully to her. Around us other stalls were rising up out of the paper and shavings covering the floor.

"Gee, that's pretty. Very festive," a Daughter exclaimed. I had placed a blue and white Wedgewood dinner service as the centre-piece and backed it with pyramids of Oxford Marmalade and Twinings tea, topped by bottles of H.P. sauce. Whisky, gin and tonic water, balanced on tins of biscuits, encircled the table. Above our heads I formed arches using cardigans, scarves and ties.

"Very artistic!" Dorrie laughed. "And what an advertisement for British exports. You should do it professionally."

I turned to the Commonwealth goods and piled up the soft Canadian blankets, their colourful stripes to the fore. I made mounds of tinned salmon and South African tinned fruits. Australian koala bears squatted in a semi-circle, and Maori necklaces, and Indian and Pakistani silver filigree jewellery swung, glittering from the bars. As a final touch brightly-coloured Commonwealth Crests dominated each Commonwealth country's goods. The raffles — a Burberry, a dinner set and a crate of beer we arranged at the corner and finally I pinned up the duty rota.

"Well, that's that." The other stalls, run by different State branches, now stretched the length of the ballroom in parallel lines, forming a brilliant display of red, green, silver and gold Christmas decorations. Dorrie and I rested on the empty crates, wiping the dirt off our faces and hands with tissues, till Alan came to fetch us.

"Hum . . . not bad. But Masha, you can't have a tiny Indian flag under a huge Union Jack."

"Why not?"

"You'll cause a diplomatic incident. They'll think it insulting."

"I asked for a four-foot flag. That's what they produced."

"You can't do it." I jumped off the crate and pushed the Indian flag angrily forward from the under the Union Jack.

"No," Alan smiled. "That's not good enough. You'll have to get a miniature Union Jack." I finally extracted one from the head waiter.

I rolled up the four-footer muttering, "You can't even see that tiny flag." The Union Jack should be the most prominent of them all, I thought. Why belittle ourselves? The Commonwealth expect us to do all the work.

The President, flushed, curls drooping, hurried up, "The detectives are here, girls. You can leave the stuff now."

Next morning Alan took me in a taxi and, with his "Good luck, dear" in my ears, I hurried in. Dorrie was already there. We took turns to watch over the stall. I strolled across to the Victoria Home booth. An elderly lady, white curls crowning a round face, beamed behind it. "We've made all these things ourselves," and she waved a hand over the stall. I looked from her mis-shapen fingers to the dainty pin-cushions, bed-socks and woolly shawls.

"Are you Mrs Williams?" she asked eagerly. We shook hands and she introduced two ladies in wheel-chairs.

"What is the Home like?" I asked.

They smiled. "It's a lovely place," one of the wheel-chair ladies answered and the other nodded. "You should see the flowers in spring. Such a colourful display and right under my window. I'm ninety, you know." She had an impish grin. Then she added, "It's a real home." Those words made our work worthwhile.

We were now surrounded by shoppers, some carrying suspiciously large shopping bags. Other booths were already selling so we started too, darting from customer to customer, keeping a wary eye on the crowd, packaging the items, cashing the money, and returning the change. We should have arranged for more help earlier.

It was hot and stuffy. There were too many people and the windows were firmly closed. Dorrie kept rubbing her forehead and my head ached too, yet the bazaar was not even officially open.

At half past twelve the first girls on the rota arrived. Daughters cleared a passage for the procession to the stage and the opening ceremony began.

Escorted by the President, whose red curls were once more piled high on her head, in sailed Lady Jebb, wife of our United Nations Ambassador. The crowd surged forward to catch a glimpse of her, and I too was eager to see our senior Foreign Service wife in New York. Her tiny figure, rigid in glistening black, chin raised, a smile fixed on a pink and white face and round doll's eyes staring ahead, she knew how to make an entrance. A sigh of satisfaction went up from the crowd. Behind her in contrast Sir Francis smiled and nodded casually, while Lady Evans had a 'when will it end' far-away look, as her escort prodded her forward. The Commonwealth C-G's wives followed.

The President's speech was inaudible to us behind a buzz of hundreds of shoppers whispering "How much?" and "I want that!" Better sell than argue, I thought, so we whispered and wrapped as speech followed speech, each — American fashion — lengthier than the last. Sir Francis' voice carried well, "It has been a privilege to help raise funds for your beautiful Victoria Home, and now I must say goodbye." His voice faded under a barrage of applause. I clapped enthusiastically, hating the thought of him leaving. Then Lady Jebb's piercing soprano rose above the hubbub and at last we heard the words, "I declare the bazaar open."

Crowds pressed round, demanding attention. The girls, flustered, whispered, "I can't find the price tag," and "There's no more tonic water," and I tried to deal with all the problems at one and the same time.

Lady Jebb, who was touring the stalls, exclaimed, "What darling bears! I'll have this one. Are you Australian?" She gave me a brittle smile. I explained who I was — the wife of a relatively junior officer. The smile disappeared; it must not be wasted. Sir Francis and Lady Evans trailed behind. Lady Evans whispered,

"Masha, you will tour the stalls, won't you? Especially the old people's." Then she smiled, "And thank you very much, dear." My headache immediately felt better.

The crowds grew dense as people came on from work. Dorrie had gone pale so we took turns to escape into the street where despite the dust and exhaust fumes we could at least inhale some air. I breathed deeply before returning. Later over a whisky in the bar I raised my glass.

"Here's to the Foreign Service. You're thrust into this sort of thing and you have to cope. Is it worth it? I suppose so. Good relations and all that, but with better organisation . . ." I drained my glass.

When Alan fetched me that evening, he told me, "By the way, the F.O. Inspectors are here."

"Whatever for? I can't cope with anything else."

"They're here to decide whether our salaries are too low or too high. I told them we could not possibly judge yet. They're not going to bother you with the bazaar going on, but is there anything you want me to tell them?"

"I don't know anything about salaries. It isn't money I'm concerned about. It's information, advice that I want. It's all so hopelessly inefficient."

As we left I kept thinking, if only there was more air. How do Americans survive without it? But one day was over, only two more to go.

Early next morning Dorrie was already at the stall and customers were prowling around. We both kept leaning against a table. Our feet and backs were a mass of aches. The crowds thickened as the day wore on.

"Honey!" The President leant across the counter — amazing woman, she seemed to be everywhere at once, "Your girls are not watching the booth. These professional thieves are quick."

It was stifling and the noise overpowering. Crowds surged past and women shouted at me, "Why isn't there any strawberry jam?" and "I've come all the way from New Jersey and now there's no Twinings tea left!"

Suddenly all these faces swayed towards me. I clutched the table. Alan, who had just arrived, exclaimed, "What's the matter?" and he took hold of my arm. "You're not going to faint?"

"No." I tried to laugh it off. "But I can't breathe here."

"Dorrie!" Alan called. She nodded, "I'll manage," and Alan drove me home.

On the third morning, too worn out to talk, we worked like automata. The bazaar was to close at eleven. I must survive till then, I told myself.

Katia came along and Wilfred, Dorrie's husband, the new Consul, a lean man with a great mop of dark hair, which he kept ruffling up with long fingers. The raffles were about to be drawn. The President suddenly annouced, "I have pleasure in introducing Mrs Williams, the new Deputy Consul-General's wife who will draw the first raffle."

I had not been warned, but up I had to go, brushing dust and shavings off my dress and there I stood on the platform facing that curious crowd with a fixed smile, my nose glistening, strands of hair falling over my eyes. I should have foreseen this. I drew several raffles, called out the numbers and then Alan took over and I escaped back to the booth.

"No. 14, Mrs Williams." I had won a dinner service! I looked up but with the chaos around me, and a pounding head, I forgot that as an official's wife I should make a gracious gesture and return the ticket for a redraw. Then it was too late. The next raffle was being drawn. I consoled myself with the thought that I had at least bought tickets from every stall.

The President passed along the stalls, "Time to drop prices, girls. Sell everything off." Thank God, it's nearly over, I thought. Dorrie and I started marking down prices. Bargain hunters fought to get to the front, grabbing socks, ties, shirts, shouting "I got it first!" "That's mine!" and there I saw my elegant sister, Katia, normally aloof, jammed against the booth, defending a set of Wedgewood plates against all buyers, buffeted but refusing to give way till the selling stopped and the auctions began. Then triumphantly she declared, "I'll have these," and paid a quarter the original price.

The auctioneer held up the last item, a cashmere sweater. I called, "Four dollars." I did not want it, but that dinner service was on my conscience.

"Five," from the other end of the hall. "Six," I shouted. "Seven." I must get it. "Eight." Silence. The sweater was mine at vastly above its value.

Alan came up, "So it was you bidding against me! It was to be a present for you." We burst out laughing.

It was past midnight as we packed up the remaining goods, while our cashier counted the proceeds.

"Alan! The South African Crest has gone!" We hunted under the booth, called the President. "I warned you," was all she said. "It was hand-painted. They sent it up specially from the South African Embassy in Washington," I could hardly control my tears. "What shall I do?"

"There's nothing you can do but write and apologise," Alan said. I had known its value and had not taken proper care of it. In silence, disheartened, and numb with exhaustion, I turned back to the packing.

Our cashier jumped up, "Our stall has made a record 2,000 dollars!" I could see that ninety-year-old lady with the impish look as Dorrie and I clasped hands and laughing we turned to our husbands, who were grinning back at us.

9

Next morning Alan escorted the Evanses to the airport.

"They looked like death warmed-up," he reported. "A colleague made a rather cruel remark, 'All that's left of Sir Francis is a gentle smile'." That hurt although I could not explain why.

We picked up some glasses and drink from their government-owned flat, a duplex in fashionable Beekman Place. We roamed through its twelve spacious rooms, empty and desolate. An enormous gilt-framed mirror over the ornate mantlepiece in the drawing-room reflected sheet-covered furniture and the litter of shavings and newspapers. The Evanses were gone. I felt sad and I burst out, "A gentle smile ... nonsense! He's exhausted, that's all. He did his best. But he'll recover." I hoped fervently that the Office would have the same sense to allow them time before their next posting.

"Jealousy," Alan smiled. "Everyone's jealous of Sir Francis. The New York Times carried an editorial on him — a rare compliment. Newspapers don't usually bother about departing consuls, and he was delighted. I asked him for a candid opinion on the job here. He laughed grimly, 'It's like being in a deep and narrow cutting with a rather large and speedy steam roller coming after you!'" I moved closer to Alan, who was pale with dark patches under his eyes. He was now acting Consul-General and I did not want him left with nothing but a gentle smile.

"Come! Let's go home," he said, "and get a bit of rest while we can." It did not occur to me that years later we would be standing on this very spot in the midst of our own disorder and shavings.

A steam roller in a narrow cutting ... Two functions a day now, seven days a week. No time for the children, for ordinary jobs such as shopping, sewing or letter-writing. Mamoo and Mary had to manage without me.

We elbowed our way into crowds at cocktail parties where

women's starkly made-up faces contrasted with their dark dresses, with silver fox or mink furs draped over their shoulders. On their heads were the most intriguingly exotic creations — a flat pancake with an enormous bow, a round disk perched over the brow and rabbit tails soaring off it. Alan could not take his eye off a mass of what looked like hat-pins bobbing up and down off a skull cap as its wearer nodded.

Rooms were over-heated; my dresses were too heavy and I perspired continually. Our main luggage had not yet arrived so I bought a black muslin dress with tiny white flowers embroidered all over a wide skirt, but next day, at the staff party, there was Dorrie, beaming, in a black muslin dress with tiny white flowers. She stopped smiling as we examined each other. Then we laughed. Out of all the numerous big stores in New York, we had to choose the same boutique. But neither of us cared and we rarely attended the same party.

The noise at cocktails was so deafening, I could not make out what was said though voices seemed loud and shrill. Mine, I guessed, by the puzzled expression on faces, was inaudible. We did not know our hosts or their guests, but New Yorkers demanded our presence for Britain was still considered a great power. As an individual I did not exist. I could only watch the spectacle before me. I stood lost and feeling foolish, hemmed in by chattering guests. I kept looking round, pretending to search for friends.

After cocktails, with aching feet and eyes smarting from cigarette smoke, we sat down to five-course dinners with politicians or bankers, up in the sky in the Rockefeller Building or in the English Grill, overlooking the skaters on the Rockefeller Plaza. Dinners with societies in luxury hotels were monster affairs. The New York Country Lawyers' Association dinner was for a thousand guests with the main speaker Governor Dewey. He had just lost the Presidential Election, it was said, because of his short stature and plump figure that lent itself so effectively for caricature.

Always different faces, in different locations, with no chance of making friends, and I never knew what to expect as every day was planned for me. I found it difficult to join in conversations for

I had little common with these monied crowds, nor had I mixed in ruling circles before, as in London we had not been included in government entertainment. It was a strange world for me.

"Is all this really necessary?" and I yawned as we left one party. I was too tired to enjoy the luxury, the distinguished speakers or the daily menu of crab meat, steaks, peach melba and chocolate soufflés. Every morning I had to dip into that precious bottle of Enos. And Alan had already had a long day's work at the office, endlessly promoting British business and reporting to our Washington Embassy on political and economic developments in New York. Also he had to be continualy available to the British community and to the local authorities. It was already too much without this late-night entertainment.

"Yes, it is," he answered yawning too. "It's important just to be seen. Britain's not popular and a face seen often becomes a 'friendly' face. We need the USA. We're in deep trouble." I nodded. The war had trained us to carry out whatever had to be done unquestioningly and it never occurred to me that the Office might be exploiting us or that we should protest. "But cheer up," Alan went on, "if we survive here and we're both pretty tough, we need never fear another posting. This is considered the most exacting!"

When American politics were discussed, I kept silent. No interference in American affairs. At one cocktail a woman shouted above the hubbub,

"Who did you vote for?"

"I'm not American. I'm British," I yelled back.

"But who would you have voted for?"

I shrugged.

"You must have an opinion."

"No, none." My preference for Truman I had to keep to myself. She mumbled something that sound very much like 'half-wit'.

At last our heavy luggage arrived and Alan took a Saturday off. From early morning till late at night, we prised open cases and unpacked, while Mary kept the children at bay and Mamoo fed us sandwiches and coffee. Out of some cases Alan made shelves for the nursery. When Lawrence bounced in from his walk, Alan pointed to them, "For your toys." Lawrence, not yet two, exclaimed, "Oh Daddy, thank you very much indeed!"

"A second Mr Polly!" Alan laughed. I hugged Lawrence and I hugged Libet. I saw so little of my babies, but Mary is kind, I thought, and Mamoo is there to cuddle them too.

With our Vienna pictures and porcelain displayed and dolls and trucks scattered around, the flat was more like home but we still did not feel settled for Alan was only a temporary Consul-General.

Suddenly newspaper-headlines shrieked, 'Third World War'. I caught my breath and read on. They reported that UN troops were falling back in Korea, and General MacArthur, that great American war hero, conqueror of the Philippines, and now UN C-in-C, was clamouring to bomb Chinese bases in Manchuria. Communism, they maintained, was threatening the whole world, and most disturbing, President Truman spoke of dropping the atom bomb in Korea. The UN to use an atom bomb! It had been formed to keep the peace and bombing the Chinese might bring Russia in! And the headline 'Third World War' meant that Americans were actually prepared to launch into war. MacArthur was a soldier, but that the ordinary American should want to fight China! At night I tossed from side to side. 'Third World War' hammered at my brain and I envied Alan, who as usual, turned on his side and fell fast asleep.

Our presence added to the general tension. Still basking in Sir Francis' popularity, we were invited everywhere but people stiffened when we were introduced. Britain was opposed to extending the war and we were protesting that MacArthur was making dangerously irresponsible statements.

"We have to go all out to get our views across," Alan said. "We have to hammer away at them. Americans think all we have to do is get out there and wipe out the Chinese and or the Russians, all those millions. They don't doubt that it can be done."

At one dinner party our host turned on me, "How can you British want communist China in the UN? You approve of communism?"

I tried to speak calmly, not to get emotional, "Every nation should be in the UN, whether it is communist or not, and that includes China, otherwise she has no obligation towards us. In the UN she would have to abide by its Charter. It's our only chance for peace. To talk. Besides, other communist countries are already there. It doesn't mean we approve of them."

"We should get out of Korea, Berlin and Europe. Leave them to settle their own problems," a guest shouted, glaring at me.

"And why shouldn't McArthur bomb China?" another interrupted.

"But the President doesn't agree . . ." I began. "It's a tug of war between the President and the General."

"Over Korea, do you really want to negotiate with China, communist China, the aggressor?" our host again attacked. Then he smiled, sat down on the couch beside me, flung an arm round my shoulders and gave my bare arm a squeeze — a friendly gesture, I realised, to soften his words. Americans constantly touched each other, but I was not used to it. I tried not to shrink from his arm on my bare back as I collected my thoughts and answered, "Yes. Surely it's better to talk than to fight, and should we cut ourselves off from a sixth of the inhabitants of the world?" Americans are so critical, I thought. They expect everyone to think and feel as they do.

I enjoyed exchanging views and as I was supposed only to express our government's opionion (I studied daily reports sent me by our Information Services), arguing had become a game that I played with this handicap. But now discussion had become deadly serious. That atom bomb . . .

It was a relief that at a St. David's Society Banquet we listened to Lord Macdonald of Gwaenysgor, "It is important to remember that negroes and communists are human beings," he teased his audience. "They have their point of view too, and there is no reason for us to fight them."

The room was still. Several hundred people and no fidgeting. "We have just won a war and to have another would interrupt the talks at the United Nations, and what should we do after we had won it? Why start talking again . . ." The audience stood up to applaud. At least these Welsh Americans do not want war, I thought.

Newspaper headlines now reported 'Congress in a Panic' and wrote that the United Nations forces 'are going to be pushed into the sea.' Mr Attlee, our Prime Minister, flew to Washington. Then he came through New York on his way for futher talks in Ottawa. Alan set off with Sir Gladwyn Jebb, our UN Ambassador, and other British officials in hired cadillacs to meet his party at the airport. I tried to read to the children while we waited for his return but my thoughts were with him, and I thought of Vania, with two young sons at university. Staring at the floor he once said, "The drafts sent to Korea are mostly untrained boys . . ."

"Well, did you see Attlee?" I sprang up as Alan came into the study.

"Yes, but I only just shook the prime ministerial hand when the charge of the press photographers began and I saw the point then of learning rugger at school." He laughed and started collecting papers off his desk.

"Then what?" I pulled at his sleeve.

"Then a press conference at which Attlee said nothing, and he was swept off to the UN." Alan picked up his brief-case. "Attlee's hat seemed too small and looked as though it might spring off his nicely polished bald head. Bye, I must run." He gave us each a quick kiss and rushed off to the office.

I could not listen to the children's chatter. Alan so flippant. Perhaps he had not had a chance to find out anything, and then he was under considerable strain. It was he who was responsible for arranging Attlee's journeys, and I also remembered that he had a habit of laughing under stress.

I could not settle down as I waited for his return from a drinks party for the P.M. at Jebb's house. At last I heard his key in the door. "What's happened?" How irritating he was, standing there, laughing to himself, "Alan!" He took off his coat slowly, then still grinning. "The P.M. met us in a bath towel! As I walked in I heard him shouting from the landing above 'Has my luggage arrived?' and there he was wrapped in a towel! He was trying to change into evening dress for dinner later." Alan was really enjoying himself. All these VIPs. But the talks with Truman must have gone reasonably well. In the study Alan helped himself to a whisky and sat down.

"But the bomb?" I wanted to shake him.

He hesitated, then, "Well, it'll be in the papers tomorrow anyway. There'll be a joint statement, but no signed agreement, that would apparently be too much for the republican opposition, but no bomb on Korea. A misunderstanding on the part of the press as to what the President meant — at least that's what he's saying. But I gather Attlee is satisfied both about the bomb and with the talks generally."

"Thank God!" I breathed and I gave him a hug.

We settled down on the couch. "What is he like? What did he say?"

"He talked about after-dinner speaking and how he enjoyed it. He thought of what he was going to say more or less as he was saying it. Someone remarked that he couldn't manage that sort of speech. Attlee said, 'It's easy for me because I learnt my speaking at street corners.'" Alan evidently appreciated that. "He's a surprisingly small man. Most unimpressive but he coped with the chaps twice his size around him. He's obviously very much respected."

Next morning Alan drove to the airport to see Attlee off, as he described it, in a cavalcade of seven cars, with police motorcyclists roaring ahead, but no sirens. These were now reserved for air-raids. Alan went on, "One of our drivers got so carried away that he roared along on the way back and caught a ticket for speeding." We laughed. It was all very satisfying and Britain evidently still had influence with the Americans.

While Alan was at the airport, I had taken the children to the zoo. They gazed into the pink gaping jaws of a hippopotamus and I taught them to say the word 'hippototamus'. Next day Vania and Nadia dropped in.

"Nadia, listen to this," and I caught hold of Lawrence. "Darling, what's the name of that big pig at the zoo?"

Lawrence grinned and announced proudly, "Attlee!" Nadia shook with laughter. 'Uncle Chocolate' tossed Lawrence into the air and caught him in his lap. I smiled; I did not think I ought to laugh.

10

At last our social duties ceased, for Christmas in New York is a family affair, and Alan had only one more task to perform — a Christmas broadcast, his first broadcast in New York. My sister, Natasha, who was staying with us, and I settled down to listen. Vania and Katia's families did the same in their homes. I was tense for it was the first time they would hear Alan in his official capacity.

His voice came over well, "In Britain Christmas is mainly for the children ..." Suddenly he was interrupted by a high-pitched voice, 'Beware of the Body Odour!' and a chorus burst into 'Avoid B.O! Avoid B.O.!' Natasha and I stared at each other, shocked, then we burst out laughing. We did not hear the rest.

When Alan came home, solemnly confident, we sang out, "Avoid B.O."

"What on earth?"

"Your sponsor," I gasped. "'Avoid B.O.' That's what they sang." Mamoo shook her head at us as we tried to control ourselves.

Alan frowned. "It's no use protesting now. I suppose this kind of vulgarity is acceptable here." His face was set as he glared at us. He's being pompous, I thought; what his mother is always afraid of. In letters to her, I always added, 'Bulletin on P (pomposity): 'Under control' or 'stable'.

"I'm an official," Alan protested.

For a whole week now we were free and were no longer officials. We would just be a family, celebrating Christmas with relations. Next morning I yawned and stretched in bed. No need to hurry, to study the diary or decide on representational clothes. I snuggled down under the bedclothes, murmuring, "We can relax now in peace with the children."

The door was flung open and Lawrence burst in, threw himself screaming to the floor banging his heels against it.

"Peace?" Alan queried.

I shouted above the yells, "At least they keep us normal. With them around there's no chance to grow pompous," and I laughed as Alan disappeared behind his airmail Times.

I lifted Lawrence on to the bed, "What is it pet?"

"Zhe 'as zhe ribbon," he wailed. Libet ran in and clambered up too, a big red bow on her hair; but she snatched it off and thrust it at Lawrence. I tied it round his head and he ran out, shouting, "Look! See!" Libet grinned and held out 'The Tale of Squirrel Nutkin'. A fair exchange, but already so cunning, I thought as obediently I began to read, 'This is the Tale about a Tail . . .' Alan mumbled something about "Peace . . ." but this is family life and he must take part in it, I thought.

Downtown, viewing the Christmas decorations, Lawrence was terrified by the Father Christmasses with bulbous noses, shaggy eyebrows and bristling moustaches at every street corner ringing bells and jingling collection boxes. He cried out, "No want Kismas!" and Alan had to drag him past them. He only cheered up on the moving staircase in Altman's where he and Libet went up and down as he shouted, "I move! I move!"

Back home at lunch Lawrence, ashamed of his fears, told Mamoo, "Kismas rings zhe bell zhere."

"Local German-Jewish accent," Alan muttered.

"Yes, Mr Bennett." (We were all avid readers of Jane Austen.) Mamoo was reproachful. Alan could mock others but not her little Lawrence.

That evening up in the Consulate, on the sixty-fourth floor of the Empire State Building, we stood rivetted, staring down at fairyland, the streets thin streaks of yellow, green lights strung over dark patches of river, and prancing, twinkling stars for miles around.

Snowflakes began to fall — a strange sight, they fell upwards.

"Daddy look!" Lawrence pressed his nose against the glass.

"It's the updraught, the air rising outside the building. It rains upwards too." The children laughed and we watched the city below gradually disappear behind the white flakes.

We weighed down the fresh, pine-smelling branches of our Christmas tree with oranges. It was customary in my family to

The three brothers-in-law, Alan, Vania, Kapa

attach the Russian white, blue and red Imperial flag to the tip, but that, I supposed, was now inappropriate and, as Alan was not demonstrative about the Union Jack, with a stab of nostalgia, I put away the Russian flag, and handed Alan a silver star.

The family had assembled in New York for the festivities. I was fortunate to have them there for members of the Foreign Service are cut off from family and friends, but I felt nervous. Alan had not yet heard my family's antiquated, ultra-conservative views. However I need not have worried; they were only concerned with family affairs.

The parties began. At the Nebolsines, for the little ones, we sang carols. Russians enjoy singing and have good voices, but this family produced a cacophony of wailing both above and below the notes. Suddenly Libet lifted her face to the Christmas tree and sang out in a rich, adult voice, perfectly in tune, 'Silent Night, Holy Night'. Everyone stopped singing. My little girl with such a voice! I listened entranced but then she started giggling.

"Go on!" the others cried, but she hid her face in my skirt and never produced that mature voice again. The cacophony started up once more and as we walked home Alan said, "Lovely Russian voices!"

At my brother Vania's Christmas Eve party we filled ourselves with turkey and cranberry sauce, sweet potatoes with marsh-mallows, and hamburgers in tomato sauce. Then we settled in armchairs and Natasha started in a clear soprano, 'Christos rodilsia', (Christ was born) — a gay little carol. Everyone joined in, singing in harmony, without accompaniment. Alan and I leant back, sipping wine and listening to the exquisite sounds that swelled and died away, and I had to blink away the tears. I was back long ago in the gold and silver of our Russian church in London in a different kind of life when, standing shoulder to shoulder, the emotional chanting of priest and choir plunged me one moment into ecstasy and the next into intense sorrow.

For Christmas I gave Alan bathroom scales — he was putting on weight. He gave me another bottle of eau-de-cologne; he must have forgotten the array of bottles he had already given me on the bathroom shelf. The children received the mass of toys I had been unable to resist.

That Christmas Day snow lay in the park. From our window the dark, bare trees, stark against the whiteness, and the tiny figures tobogganing down the slopes in brilliant sunshine made it a real Bruegel. The younger Nebolsines, Arkadi and Katiousha, arrived with sledges, and with our children on their backs, they careered down the icy slopes of the hillock outside our windows. I was touched that these youngsters should give so much time and attention to our little ones. All four returned for tea with bright red cheeks and sparkling eyes.

"What? No Russian flag on the Christmas tree?" Arkadi asked.

"No, I'm British now."

"Well, at least England is a monarchy, though it does have a Labour government." Russians fall naturally into discussion and argument.

"I can't understand that," Katiousha's large grey eyes stared at us earnestly. "How can English people choose Labour? Labour is atheist. Without the church there are no morals."

Libet and Lawrence in Central Park, 1951

"You're simplifying," Alan began.

"Democracies are rotten anyway," Arkadi stated. "Monarchy, our Russian model with the Orthodox Church supreme — that's the answer."

"It failed in Russia," Alan was patient. They were thoughtful, but Arkadi always had an answer, "That's because of the war." How strange to hear such opionions in contemporary USA. I had grown up with them but these youngsters were third generation refugees.

When they left Alan said, "Well, they're young still. They'll learn to think for themselves." I was relieved. He was not put out by my family's views.

Next day as the family poured in for our Christmas dinner Alan amused himself by greeting each one — Russian style — by their name and patronym.

"Hellow Ekaterina Lavrentievna! Hello Arkadi Rostislavovitch! Ekaterina Rostislavna! ..." As Arkadi handed him a special present, everyone laughed: it was a bottle labelled 'Avoid B.O,'

Over the twenty-five pound turkey, Mamoo beamed at the family, sixteen of us, gathered round the table, all under her wing and she raised her glass to propose the traditional toast, 'Absent friends and relations!'

"Bottoms up!" and Natasha downed her vodka.

"Really Natashenka!" Mamoo was shocked and she was puzzled when we laughed.

We over-ate, paper hats on our heads, British fashion, while crackers frightened the children. We shouted out silly jokes and mottoes. Vania snatched a juicy turkey leg off young Vassik's plate (Natasha's son). Vassik tried to grab it and Lawrence jumped for it too. Vania was at home with children. Meanwhile Mamoo kept piling more food on every plate.

Then over fortunes we craned forward, cheeks red from the wine and voices loud, and in turn we held a tablespoonful of wax over a candle. We dropped it into a basin of cold water, the wax solidified and the strange shadows it threw on to the wall foretold our future. Vassik held up what looked like a hand with a stick.

"He's getting a beating," Vania chuckled.

Mamoo's fortune looked like a moon. "Romance!" Natasha breathed.

We played characters. Alan was supposed to act 'cheeky', but he was no actor. He waved his hand and murmoured under his breath.

"You're hopeless," the others cried. Alan was self-conscious and hated parlour games, but he felt at home among his new relations and merely laughed.

That night Mamoo drew me aside, "I'm so happy that Alan accepts them all," she whispered as she kissed me good-night.

"I am two old!" Lawrence bounced in on December 29th, his birthday. The family rallied round, cousins, uncles, aunts arrived with presents. We played Ring-a-Ring-a-Roses. We sang 'Oranges and Lemons', Libet insisting on holding hands with Katiousha so that Vania, too tall to stoop under their arms, hurled her high over his head as he went under and she shrieked with joy. Libet was as self-conscious as her father, but she climbed all over these relations. That evening when I tucked her up in bed, she heaved a deep blissful sigh and I sighed with her — so many relations and so much affection for all of us, Alan, me and the children. What did their views matter?

Xana, the elder Nebolsine daughter, was to give her New Year's Eve party in our flat. The Nebolsines arrived early to prepare the food. In the kitchen Kapa spread himself over the whole table to prepare his 'zakusky', leaving only one corner for Katia and Katiousha to make their meat balls. Arkadi, tucking into a salt cucumber, continued an argument.

"I still say we should get out of Korea and out of Europe . . ."

"We can't," Kapa interrupted, and suddenly they were all shouting.

Kapa: "I distrust . . ."

Natasha: "The communists would destroy . . ."

Katiousha: "Nonsense, Papa. The Germans . . ."

Mamoo: "Quiet! I disagree . . ."

Alan stole out of the kitchen, muttering, "Sounds like a fair-sized riot . . ." I laughed and went on cutting sandwiches. I could no longer compete.

That night an envelope was slipped under our door. Alan opened it and sat heavily down on the couch.

"What is it?"

"From our Information Services. They want me to deliver a sermon."

"A sermon?" He nodded. I flopped down beside him convulsed with laughter. "Where?" I gasped.

"In the Church of Heavenly Rest, on Fifth Avenue," and he added gloomily, "The most fashionable in town."

Full of good food and wine and still thinking of all the affection surrounding us, I felt sure that starting the year with a sermon would bring us good fortune. But seeing Alan's agonised face, I burst out laughing again.

11

The Rector led us in to the vast church. The congregation of dark-coated men, and women in mink and sable, was seated in lines of straight hard pews, the austerity relieved only by heavy-headed crysanthemums far away on the altar steps and poinsettias, echoes of Christmas, on the altar itself. As we advanced solemnly past the pews I felt exposed, with none of the warm security of a Russian church. I was painfully self-conscious and heads, turning surreptitiously to glimpse our faces, threw me into a panic. We stepped into the long, empty front pew and knelt for the moment's prayer. Then as we stood up the organ roared out the first hymn, the congregation competed and a lady's shrill soprano quivered in the air behind us.

A procession swung slowly down the aisle, headed by the clergy and followed by men and women of the British and Commonwealth 'Patriotic Societies', the ex-servicemen stiff in khaki and blue uniforms, carrying banners with 'St George', 'St Andrew', 'St David', 'Daughters of the British Empire', emblazoned in gold lettering and underneath 'The Bronx', 'Brooklyn' and other districts of New York. They saluted before the altar, parted and stood the banners along the white walls on either side.

The evening service began. I clutched the hymn book in sweaty hands and, fighting for calm, tried to breathe deeply. Alan stood motionless, his hands steady around the 'Order of Service'.

Why must I be so nervous? I wondered. Understandable when I'm performing in public, but why suffer for Alan too? I hardly heard the service. People here are friendly; they've invited our British societies; it's an honour for Alan to act for the Consul-General and an opportunity to speak for his country, so why can't I enjoy it? My hands trembled.

The singing stopped, the organ wheezed to a halt. The rector marched down towards us, bowed to Alan and gestured for him to step out. In morning dress Alan looked stately and very official. He climbed slowly up into the pulpit. The congregation sat down. I was alone in the pew, but there's nothing to worry about; if he dries up, loses his voice, tomorrow will be just the same. How I longed for that tomorrow! I forced myself to look up at Alan. His hands clutched the sides of the pulpit. His face was pale but he hardly glanced at the notes in front of him. That morning I had gone secretly into the little Russian church, round the corner from us, with its blue onion dome and golden cross. It was the Russian Christmas, thirteen days later by the old calendar, and listening to the singing, so deeply moving, I had prayed that all should go well.

Alan's voice sounded remote. I caught the words, "corporate worship . . . feeling of being at home in this church . . ." Hardly! But stop thinking about yourself. I tried to listen. "This is a bewildering country. One has a feeling of being in a completely strange land . . ." True. Then followed what that congregation must have longed to hear, "but occasions such as today, when one is aware of a warm and sympathetic welcome, give an insight into the true friendship which exists between our countries . . ."

Then Alan related how a Russian officer in Vienna had plied us with questions about the West and how his first question had been 'We in the Soviet Union live for the State, what do you live for?' Alan was braving McCarthyism and the American hatred of all things Soviet! He was making this Soviet officer's question the main theme of his address! Good for him! "The difference between the communist ideal and our democratic system, whose basis is an ethical standard rooted in Christian teaching, is that one of our main purposes . . . is the full development of the individual under the rule of self-discipline, and not the individual for the State." Yes, I thought, self-discipline but that's where our system fails. We no longer teach it and we no longer practise it.

Alan always maintained that the clergy are actors and he thought it unfair that he could neither answer nor argue with clergymen in their pulpits. Now here he was in full flow, leaning forward as though embracing the congregation in his out-stretched arms, acting out his own part. "Each individual," his voice rang out, "Should ask himself 'What do I live for?' since it is from the individual's will, from his concept of an ideal civilisation, that the conduct of national life takes shape." Suddenly I was with him, I forgot myself as I listened eagerly. "It is the responsibility of each one of us to see that our democratic ideal is maintained. Instead therefore of knowing that there is a state authority which will discipline our shortcomings, we have the more arduous task of keeping ourselves up to the mark." The congregation was still. There was no fidgeting.

Then he turned to our official line and cited the 'corporate achievement' of Marshall Aid and how through hard work and austerity, Britain had managed to suspend it nearly two years earlier than planned. I sat straight, head high, proud of my country, carried away by Alan's ringing voice and the hushed crowd behind me. Alan quoted the Chancellor of the Exchequer, "We are not an emotional people ..." (No? My throat had contracted) "but this should not be allowed to hide the profound sense of gratitude towards the American people for the material help and for the spirit of understanding and friendship in which it has been given." These warm-hearted people ...

Turning to the Korean war, Alan quoted Mr Attlee on our determination to 'stand by our friends, confident that we have neglected no opportunity for a peaceful and honourable settle- ment of the dispute.' That threw my thoughts into disarray. Was the war really our concern? Shouldn't the Koreans settle it for themselves? But how? It was the Great Powers who set up the two Koreas. Doubts again ... I stifled them quickly. I must toe the line. Alan went on, "Let us be sure that each of us does his utmost to fit himself for the difficult time ahead." I sighed. If only we could improve relations with the Soviet Union and get together with the other communist countries. We all profess the same aims; to better everyone's lot. But at least, I decided, we can do our bit here in the USA to preserve good relations.

Alan had fallen silent. Panic! Had he dried up? He could finish now. But he started again, speaking slowly, deliberately. "Great qualities of leadership are demanded of us which we must be able and ready to give. If we make this our New Year resolution to become confident in effort ..." He raised his voice and leant towards us, "modest in success, gracious in defeat, fair in anger," and now louder, "of clear judgement even in the bitterness of wounded pride and ready for service at all times, we shall have done our part as individuals for the improvement of this world." He seemed to tower over us as his voice rang out in Churchill's words, "I avow my hope and faith, sure and inviolate, that in the days to come the British and American peoples will walk together in majesty, in justice and in peace."

Alan was back beside me. He's enjoyed that, I thought, as the congregation drowned the organ with 'God Save the King' and 'The Star Spangled Banner'.

It was over. I smiled with relief as the Rector led us to the door with a "Thank you. We're grateful," and the crowd jostled to reach us and shake our hands. We beamed as they said, "I appreciate the message in your sermon," "Excellent! Excellent!" and "Thank you. I shall always remember it." One man informed us that "My father once knew a man from Wales called Williams." Another gentleman caught my arm, "I never told my children what we live for and now it's too late."

"No, it's never too late," I replied.

Back home Mamoo exclaimed, "It should have been a bit more religious."

"Why? How do you know?"

"I sneaked in at the back." She laughed. "I'm glad I went. It was good."

As we relaxed over the evening whisky, Alan sighed, "At least that's done!" I quoted, 'modest in success . . .' We grinned at each other and at the end of that week's letter to his parents, I added, 'Bulletin on P in spite of success of sermon, still stable.'

12

There was no sign of a new Consul-General. We had to continue as 'Acting C-G' and wife throughout the season's public functions, and as Alan put it, we had to 'keep alive American interest in all things British'. I was ready to do my bit but I wasn't prepared for the extraordinary situations awaiting us.

We set out one evening, I in a new black taffeta evening gown under my musquash, to attend the première of a British film — a gala performance with the Mayor present, the Chief of Police, film stars and, I thought complacently, ourselves.

Alan and Paula Edden, who had just joined our Information Services accompanied us. Paula wore a new black lace creation under a short mink jacket.

As we drove up searchlights pierced the sky and an enormous crowd surrounded the theatre. The promoters had evidently been very successful. But there was no way through that crowd. The police had forgotten to clear a passage for the guests. We got out of the car and faced a solid wall of backs.

"So much for American efficiency," Alan exclaimed. In all our finery we, the official guests, had to fight our way through the throng. Setting their shoulders to the backs, our husbands shoved. There was a gleam of excitement in Alan's eye: he could legitimately use his muscle. There were cries of 'Hey, you guys, cut it out. Stop pushing.' I clung to Alan's sleeve and slid into the gaps he made, dragging a resisting Paula after me, while she protested,

"This isn't right! We shouldn't have to . . ." After struggling through to the front we faced a police cordon — two thick ropes strung around the theatre.

"This is too much," Alan Edden protested, hair hanging over his eyes.

"Come on!" and Alan started climbing through.

"Hey you there, get back!" Policemen in square-shouldered heavy overcoats and gleaming brass buttons, ran up.

"Are we supposed to fly in then?" Alan retorted. Taken aback the police rushed around seeking instructions. The two men held the ropes apart and, bent double, we lifted our long skirts above our knees and climbed through straight into the blinding television lights and cameras. Quickly we straightened our hair and clothes and composed ourselves. Paul hissed into my ear, "Look! There's a great tear in my dress, my lovely lace. It's a disgrace!" I sympathised but with the cameras on my face I was trying hard to control my laughter.

At last inside the cinema, I walked ahead along a corridor when a woman darted up to me and pushed what looked like a jam pot under my chin.

"Tell the folks what it all looks like." An empty corridor, not even a bowl of flowers.

"It's . . . it's all lovely," I blurted out, pushing the jam pot aside. A member of our Information Services ran up, seized it and shouted into it,

"Mrs Williams is looking forward to seeing this fascinating film about our police forces . . ." I bit my lip. Of course, it was a microphone.

During the film Paula kept muttering, "It's the limit. I shall sue them. My lovely dress." Evidently, I thought, we must always be prepared for the unexpected, but how?

Next we were invited to the one hundred and twenty fifth anniversary of the Old Guard of the city of New York, that is, the New York State militia. The ballroom of the Hotel Commodore was packed with dancing couples. Accustomed to our own solemn military occasions, we had expected something austere, martial; but here were a host of elderly gentlemen jogging along to a lively fox-trot, dressed up in gloriously colourful eighteenth-century uniforms, red and blue jackets and white trousers with tall, shiny, black helmets, and they were wearing swords.

After gazing at them in astonishment, I seized Alan's hand, "Let's dance too. Please!" He glanced quickly round. There were no officials to greet us. He whirled me on to the dance floor. It was well polished, the drums beat out a strong rhythm, Alan was light and quick on his feet. We had more or less danced into matrimony in Vienna, but ever since there had been no opportunity and I longed to dance.

We raced up and down the ballroom, and I held tight to his shoulder as he swung me round this way and that. It was a glorious interlude but then the music stopped. We stood flushed, laughing till we noticed groups of men collecting for what looked like a Grand Review, and at the end of the hall, VIPs were being introduced to a reviewing General in regular army uniform. We hurried guiltily across, shook his hand and were led up into a box in the gallery where we settled demurely down to watch the march-past.

Drums throbbed, bands started up, standards waved and uniformed veterans of World War I and II marched past. I nudged Alan. The ancient gentlemen in fancy uniform were shuffling along too, clinging to heavy, weaving flag poles. An army officer beside us whispered, "The old men like an excuse to dress up."

"It's harmless," Alan whispered back.

Our British ex-servicemen, who mostly had dual nationality and extended their patriotism across both countries, marched in battle dress, behind the Union Jack. To our relief, in spite of our British criticism of General MacArthur in Korea, they were applauded as enthusiastically as the rest. Finally the Parade Commander stepped forward, a frail, ancient figure. His tall helmet wobbled on a shaking head. He saluted and his drawn sword trembled dangerously close to the General's nose. He managed to pull it back to safety and staggered off. Our military friend murmured, "Looks like he joined the organisation about the date of its formation." It was fantastic, old men playing at soldiers, but the veterans were not put out and the General stood stiffly at the salute.

I enjoyed the evening. The old men were childish but why shouldn't they be, and mercifully the New York militia did not appear to be warlike.

Then came a meeting of the Daughters of St George, a society of sober matrons, I imagined. But what we walked into was a gathering of elderly ladies in white robes, high-necked and long-sleeved, their startling make-up caked on to their lined and wrinkled faces. Clutching long, peach-coloured gladioli, they grinned and chattered. I joined Wilfred Thomas, our Consul, and Dorrie, his wife, on the dais. Both avoided looking at me as they rose to greet me, and knowing that I must not laugh, I avoided their eyes. The ladies in white lined up in couples, raised their gladioli aloft and formed an arch. A very aged Grand President, tall and gaunt, slipped her arm through Alan's. 'Rule Britannia' resounded through the hall, thumped out by a lady at a piano, and Alan and the President tripped briskly round the room. They dived between the white ladies and under the arch of gladioli. The sight of Alan, so retiring and yet imposing in his dark, discreet suit, emerging with his frail old lady from their flowery bower, was almost too much for me. I stared fixedly at the floor. Dorrie's plump shoulders heaved and her face disappeared into her handkerchief. The piano chords crashed fortissimo and the couple swept off round the room again, disappearing between the white ladies and under the gladioli. As they emerged a second time, Alan, an experienced consular officer, who could be relied on to take most things in his stride, suddenly let out a loud guffaw. Our consular group stiffened and we looked quickly at the President, but she pressed Alan's arm, gazed up at him and laughed. All the white ladies laughed with her and to our relief we were able to join in.

The ladies then lined up; those to the fore carried banners and their President addressed them. American women fill in time with their speeches and say nothing worth remembering, I was thinking as Alan rose to speak. He had been chortling to himself and now suddenly he began reciting:

"I like a finished speaker
I mean I really do.
I don't mean one that's polished,
I mean the one that's through."

Tremendous applause. The ladies beamed and it was some time before Alan could continue. When he finally sat down the President announced, "Now Mrs Williams will say a few words." I started, then stood up. This was unexpected. I was not prepared. Silence. All eyes were on me. In a panic, I blurted out what was in my mind.

"In England we're taught to speak only when we have something of particular interest to impart." But what was I to impart? I looked round desperately. Something momentous, or at least interesting . . . Nothing came to mind. "So . . . Well, I wish you all the best in your charitable work and thank you for inviting us."

Dorrie uttered what sounded like a snort.

"It wasn't right, Alan," I grumbled later. "If they had warned me, I would have thought of something encouraging to say."

"In the USA you must always be ready to speak. Always have a few thoughts prepared."

"Why didn't you warn me? I never know what's expected of me!"

"Well, I mean, wives . . . I never thought wives would be involved." Before I could protest, he burst into uncontrollable laughter. "Those ladies in white . . . and the gladioli . . ." Then he added more soberly, "But they were good sports. They might well have taken offense when I laughed." Dignity . . . Maybe we attach too much significance to dignity. Perhaps we should remain youthful too . . .

13

There was still no C-G's wife so I had to perform certain of the duties that would have fallen to her. I now knew that Americans are unpredictable and that my official status did not guarantee that things would run according to plan. I launched into them with trepidation.

N.B.C. wished to interview me and I was driven to the studio for a rehearsal. I had never broadcast before, let alone live. Before going in, I took deep breaths as I had learnt to do to control my nerves. The interviewer told me he would discuss our previous postings, the British Foreign Service and the wife's role in it. I agreed, and back home I prayed for the intervening days to pass quickly.

My sister, Natasha, was again staying with us. When the ominous day arrived and I had set out for the studio, as she told me later, she tuned in well in advance to be sure not to miss my broadcast. A British journalist was being interviewed.

"What do you think of New Yorkers?"

"They're impossibly rude. They push you about; they've no time for anyone but themselves."

"So as a visitor, are you saying, Sir, that you don't find them helpful?"

"Yes, quite the contrary. They tread all over you in their haste."

Natasha was annoyed. It was hardly polite to speak frankly. Meanwhile in the car, hot and cold in turns, I was trying to collect ideas — the dust storms in Baghdad, the rioting . . .

The interview came to an end. Mrs Williams, the acting British Consul-General's wife was announced. I braced myself and clung to the table between me and the interviewer.

"Mrs Williams, did you enjoy your previous assignments?"

"Yes. Very much. We were in Vienna first. We were married

there and then we were sent to Baghdad, where our children were born."

Then suddenly, "As a foreign visitor, what do you think of New Yorkers?"

"I'm amazed how polite and helpful they are."

He stared at me. "Really? Polite and helpful. In what way?"

"Well, I tried to post a letter in your 'trash can'. Passers-by though they were hurrying to work, stopped and pointed out the 'U.S. Mail'. When I hesitated before a crowded, revolving door, spinning rapidly, people stood back and slowed it down for me. New Yorkers are in a permanent hurry; life goes on so fast, but they make time to help a stranger."

The interview was not proceeding as planned, but there was no time to think. I was two people, one cringing inside with nervousness, the other answering calmly, amazed that my brain worked automatically.

"So, you actually find them helpful?"

"Very. If I go into the wrong shop, they don't just say that they do not have what I want, they tell me where I can find it. And liftmen, taximen explain how to get to places."

He plied me with questions that I did not expect, and Natasha was delighted; I contradicted everything the journalist had said. When it was over I sat breathing heavily, my face flushed. I was surprised when the interviewer thanked me profusely and I wondered why he was amused.

"That was great. Thank you, thank you very much." Back home Natasha, laughing too, explained.

I had managed rather well. I was pleased with myself, smug. I can do as well as any C-G's wife, I thought, and I faced the next challenge with confidence.

Mrs Otis, a wealthy American, gave generously to British charities and to encourage her further, I attended a luncheon she gave in her luxury hotel suite. Twenty women foregathered in a spacious drawing-room, the windows draped in heavy red velvet curtains and armchairs upholstered in red velvet too. Massive glass-fronted cabinets displayed Meissen porcelain and heavy silver platters. In the midst of it all, Mrs Otis sat on a couch. She looks like a toad, I thought, encased in black, squat, with a round, bloated face and black hair plastered down on either side of a straight centre parting. Her swollen legs hung down wide apart, fat feet forced into high-heeled patent leather shoes.

As we shook hands, she gazed intently, with dark bulging eyes into my face and held on to my hand, drawing me down towards her. I pulled away as she whispered, "You shall sit next to me at lunch." The Canadian C-G's wife and a Minister's wife from Washington were senior to me, and etiquette dictated that I should be seated further down the table. But as she limped, leaning on a silver-topped stick, into the dining-room, maids were changing the place-names, and to my intense discomfort, I found myself on her right, set aside from the other women, who, to my dismay, accepted it — a privileged guest.

Over the hors-d'ouevre she leered at me, "We must be friends. I hope you like me." I did not.

With the soup, I turned as was customary, to the guest on my right, but Mrs Otis, after a cursory remark to her other neighbour, called to me, "My dear, tell me all about yourself." I could not ignore her, my hostess, though I did not want to tell her anything. I ate slowly, leaving little time for conversation.

At last the meal was over. I hung back as Mrs Otis led the way to the drawing-room. "Mrs Williams, come, my dear! But I can't go on calling you Mrs Williams. Masha's your name, isn't it? You don't mind?" I did, but we walked out together, Mrs Otis leaning on my arm. She stroked my wrist. How ridiculous, I thought, and hoped that the others had not noticed. Had I somehow misled her? I tried to disengage my arm.

She drew me down beside her on the sofa, her sagging rouged cheeks, blinking eyes and half-parted scarlet lips close to my face. I shivered, shrank from her, and pulled my hand away from the soft, clutching fingers. I looked round for someone to distract her, to let me get away, but the other women, after that superb luncheon rested contentedly in their arm-chairs, chatting over coffee.

It's too silly, I thought, but what am I to do? I tried to get out of her reach by leaning forward and admiring the exquisite knick-knacks in a glass case, a collection of miniature silver animals — a camel, an elephant, a kangaroo. Mrs Otis exclaimed, "I know I own a lot of treasures, but I love presents. You can give me anything, however modest. I'd appreciate that." What a rapacious woman, I thought, staring appealingly at Mrs Green, the senior lady. But etiquette had been undermined by my placement at lunch and Mrs Green continued to sip her coffee.

I jumped up, "I'm sorry, but I must go. My husband's waiting," and I hurried out.

"I'm never going there again," I burst out to Alan. "She's repulsive, horrid!"

"Made a pass at you, did she?" and Alan grinned. And yet she gives generously, I had to remind myself.

After the shock of Mrs Otis I was not so keen on attending my next function. At an Annual Awards Breakfast of the American Mothers' Committee I was to deliver a message from Lady Albemarle who had agreed to be the United Kingdom's Mother. I had never attended such a big function without Alan. But I could not now refuse.

"What do I have to do?" I asked Alan nervously.

"Get Lady Albemarle's speech from the President ... apart from that I don't really know ..." That wasn't very helpful.

In an ante-room of the Waldorf Astoria the United Nations Mothers were being lined up in alphabetical order. As I awaited my turn, I heard sniffing. A dark young woman beside me held a handkerchief to a childish face and her shoulders heaved.

"What is it?" I whispered. "What's the matter?"

She sobbed out, "Jewish women ... questions ... 'Why this? Why that?' I don't know. I know nothing." And as I looked at her with astonishment, she added, "I'm Jordanian." Yes, those huge, black mascaraed eyes and that hennaed hair, while most of the organisers looked Jewish. An Arab alone among Jews and she looked about nineteen. Our children were born in Baghdad. Iraq and its Arabs were dear to me, but though I had never been to Israel, I felt at home among Jews too. How complicated life is, I thought, and I sighed and pressed the young woman's hand. "Never mind. Take no notice. You're their guest. If anyone objectionable, just say that you'll leave." She wiped her eyes and leant up against me.

"Argentina! Bolivia! Here please! Where has Bolivia got to?" A smartly-dressed woman was propelled towards the line. "Please stand here. Brazil! Now where's Brazil? Here please. No, Bolivia don't move." The organiser grabbed Bolivia's arm. "Chile! Peru! Uruguay!" The ladies remained in place for a second or two, then "Ah, Señora, como esta?" and off they sped to greet each other. It was chaos; only we, well-disciplined northerners remained in line. I began to enjoy myself.

"Italy! Spain! Please, please stand still." The line broke. Women rushed about embracing each other. The organiser's voice was drowned. Desperate, arms spread out to restrain several mothers at once, she suddenly shouted, "I can't control them. They won't stay put. Help, someone!" Assistants rushed forward and eventually we mothers were pushed and held in place.

We filed into the banqueting hall. A long dais in the centre of the room was surrounded by small tables at which the Mothers from the American States and their guests were seated. They rose and the hubbub subsided as we, United Nations Mothers, took our seats on the dais. There was only just room for the table and chairs, with a dangerous few inches between the backs of the chairs and the edge of the dais. We climbed sideways on to the dais so as not to fall off. On my left the place-card stated: 'Mother Yugoslavia'. I turned to a distinguished gentleman in a light grey suit with a pale, narrow face and slender hands.

"How do you do, Mother Yugoslavia" and I held my hand out.

"How do you do? But why do you say that?" I pointed to his place-card,

"It's a mistake." He waved his hands in alarm. "I'm the Consul-General. My secretary must have misunderstood."

I laughed. "Well, you've walked into a Mothers' gathering. I represent Mother United Kingdom."

"You must help me. Please! Tell me what to do." I shrugged. I did not know either except that he must speak on behalf of the mothers of his country. "As here you are now Mother Yugoslavia!" We grinned at each other.

"Tell me, how is it that you pronounce 'Yugoslavia' as we do?" I hesitated, then admitted, "I'm Russian born."

"I have Russian blood in me too, and Bulgarian."

"Bulgarian! My grandmother was Bulgarian. My great-grandmother was a Karavelov." The Karavelovs had led Bulgaria against the Turks and I was proud of the fact.

"But I'm also connected to the Karavelovs." He was excited, he raised his voice and pressed my hand. "We're relations, or at least, connected." We laughed, absorbed in ourselves, Slavs together. But we had attracted attention. American mothers at nearby tables turned and frowned at me, their mouths hard lines of disapproval. Suddenly I understood, he was from behind the Iron Curtain, a communist, and I was not supposed to associate with communists, and with all these Americans watching ... and McCarthy ... My companion was smiling at me. Dogmas, theories, religious, political, I thought, I'm caught up in them. But they're all divisive, they breed hatred, and inwardly I protested, it's the individual who counts, and counts above everything else. Besides I've been invited here and placed next to my companion; I have to be polite. I ignored the black looks and smiled back.

"Ladies and Gentlemen ..." The President of the American Mothers was on her feet, a portly 'Miss Mary H. Hughes' according to the programme. Amercians are full of surprises.

And now the crab meat smothered in mayonnaise lying snugly on a lettuce leaf on my plate remained untouched. The speeches were about to start and my stomach was heaving. "Will the United Nations Mothers please come up in turn." Mother Argentina pushed her chair back to rise and with a loud scraping it tumbled off the dais, carrying her with it — a mass of waving arms and silk-clad legs. She was helped up in silence and was led to the microphone where she struggled through her speech in broken English. Then the Belgian too toppled backwards off the dais; strange, she had seen Argentina fall. Brazil stumbled but managed to save herself. Mother Pakistan rose to her feet and turned out to be an immense dark man with huge moustaches, but he thought fast and began, "On behalf of my mother, who was unable to attend ..."

"That's you cue," I whispered to Mother Yugoslavia. "Speak on behalf of your mother or wife."

My turn was approaching. My heart was pounding. "Mother United Kingdom!"

My head was in a whirl. I pushed back my chair and flew off the dais landing up against Mother Yugoslavia, who had risen just in case, and now held me. With his laughter in my ears, blushing and confused, I made my way to the head of the table. "My speech," I remembered to whisper to the President. She thrust papers into my hands.

I stood before the microphone. "Ladies and Gentlemen," and I began reading. "Would Her Majesty agree ..." I stopped. A request to the Queen to be Mother United Kingdom. I flicked the page over and began again, "Her Majesty regrets ..." I stopped again and there I stood, hundreds of rows of faces gazing up at me, waiting, and a whole sheaf of papers in my hands, but where among them was my speech? I had to keep talking. You can't stand silent before a microphone. As I leafed through the pages, I improvised, "As Mother United Kingdom, Lady Albemarle has great pleasure ..." a request to Princess Elizabeth ... a refusal ... "in sending you her greetings ..." A request to Princess Margaret ... Hurriedly I turned the pages. Ah, at last. Here it was. Breathless, I stumbled through Lady Albemarle's speech and was able to hurry back to my seat.

Mother Yugoslavia was already standing. No risk of his falling. I whispered, "Good Luck!" and sat down. He began, "On behalf of my wife ..." I hid behind my programme, hoping no-one would see me heaving with laughter.

When the speeches were over and the Awards made, we stood up, a lighted candle in our hands to receive a Rabbi's blessing — a reminder that New York was not so much Irish as Jewish, but a blessing, I thought, is welcome from whatever quarter. I peered up the table and saw that Mother Jordan was obligingly holding her candle too.

"What we do for our country" I murmoured as I said goodbye to Mother Yugoslavia.

"I enjoyed it," he laughed. Then he bent down and kissed my hand in front of all the American mothers. "Good-bye, Mother United Kingdom!"

14

I was improvising without help or instruction and as a result I was continually keyed up. No-one can stand such strain for long. But now we were to call on Sir Oliver, the British Ambassador (or H.E as he was referred to) and Lady Franks, in Washington. There I would meet the Embassy wives. I would benefit from their experience, get their advice; we could compare notes and I would extract from them all that they had learnt about serving in the USA.

It was only four hours by train to Washington. I stared eagerly out of the window for my first glimpse of the countryside but it was flat, dismal and smelly, starting with the Newark factory area, and stretching from refinery to tannery.

But Washington, or what I saw of it from the car that met us, was a city of broad, tree-lined avenues, straddling the Potomac, and it was under a spacious sky, unencumbered by New York's sky-scrapers.

My colleagues lived in small, charming houses with shrub-filled gardens. I launched immediately into a series of coffee parties at which Ministers' wives, dressed with American elegance, entertained me while Alan did the round of the Embassy office. He was back in a familiar Foreign Office atmosphere; he met and consulted with colleagues he had known in Iceland, the Congo, Hamburg. He found Washington a pleasanter city with none of New York's hysterics and scare-headlines.

We were invited to mixed buffet lunches at which we were served my favourite crabmeat, and peach melbas, and to dinner in evening dress with candles lighting up elegant furnishings. We were to meet as many of the huge Embassy staff as possible.

I was among Foreign Service wives of my own rank. They told me that in Washington they were able to make numerous friends for they mixed all the time in the same political circles, meeting the same people and not continually among strangers as we were in New York. They had time for their children. The Minister with whom we stayed came home for lunch, and, after work, played with his two-year old daughter. He had time for square dancing for exercise; he was not out on duty every night. I could not help feeling jealous.

Though I basked in the warm welcome we were given, I was impatient to question the wives about clothes, climate, and what was expected of me at the different functions at which I so often felt out of my depth. I also planned to discuss how we could pass the useful information we acquired to our successors.

At last a suitable moment arrived as we wives sat primly over morning coffee and chocolate éclairs. I began,

"In a new post one never knows what is expected of one . . ."

"That makes it all the more exciting," a wife laughed. "Keeps you on your toes, teaches you to take things in your stride."

"But it's so taxing . . ."

"Well, if you can't stand the pace . . ." another wife began and someone muttered "If you can't stand the heat, stay out of the kitchen." They fell silent and I sat feeling very inadequate. But I persisted, "It's so easy to pass on information, to help each other . . ." Then I fell silent as they looked away. My hostess turned to me, "Have some more coffee, and do have another éclair."

I felt obliged to laugh it all off as I shook my head and added quickly, "Of course, it's all fun too."

"Some people always find things to complain about," another wife remarked. I felt rebuked and said no more. I had transgressed some Foreign Service custom. Yet they must have their troubles, I thought. Those dark patches under their eyes, the stifled yawns at dinner, the little nervous gestures. Are they afraid of being considered weak, or dare they not admit, even to themselves, that too much is expected of them, for fear of breaking down?

My hostess turned to me, "What was your last posting?"

"Baghdad. You should see it! You're buried under dust storms! You breathe, eat, cough and sneeze sand!" I did not mention the riots or the killings. I too could laugh at my troubles!

"In Panama you wallow in perspiration; it streams down you

permanently."

"We're sitting on a marsh right here in Washington." So we continued to joke. I was deeply disappointed and puzzled. However we still had not called on Sir Oliver and Lady Franks. Perhaps Lady Franks might be helpful.

Alan was nervous. "Sir Oliver is reputed to have a brilliant brain," he sighed as he went off. I was even more nervous, afraid of saying or doing the wrong thing. An Ambassardress was such a superior being and the Embassy Residence was awesome with vistas of long corridors and huge rooms, spread over a vast area.

Lady Franks, a large, homely woman in a twin set and without make-up, leaned back in a cushioned arm-chair. Sir Oliver, she told me, refused all entertainments between five and seven, a time set aside for their children. But how could we do that in New York with all the cocktail parties? She shrugged. The Franks were not regular Foreign Service and they behaved as they pleased. Lady Franks was calm and relaxed, fresh from an orderly life in Britain. She chatted on and gave me no opportunity to discuss any problems. I sat and listened, thinking disconsolately that the call was useless, the whole trip was pointless. I felt disheartened, but I did not tell Alan, for he was pleased with his interview. Sir Oliver had told him to get on with his job as he thought best, which was how he liked to work.

Only on our last evening in Washington before going to dinner did we manage to fit in a quick tour of the Capitol and the other public buildings. They were closed for the night, but their white marbles facades and pillars gleamed majestically in the flood-lighting. It was impressive and beautiful.

It had been refreshing to be out of New York and I told Alan in the train that I had enjoyed the trip, but then I ventured to add, "The wives didn't want to discuss ways of helping each other, organising something . . ."

"No-one likes change," he mused. "Better to stick it out — that's the general attitude." I changed the subject wondering at the same time whether I too was now afraid of showing weakness or of being labelled a grumbler. I'm lucky to be in New York, I thought, away from all those wives; I'm not really a social animal, and Washington is all politics. We don't fit into that scene. Then I laughed to myself. Washington wives don't attend Old Guard Balls, or get involved with the Mothers of America. As the train drew in, I said to Alan, "I'm glad we're here." Alan nodded.

15

Henry Hobson was to be the new Consul-General. We drove to the docks to meet him and his wife, wondering nervously, would they be aloof, difficult? The Queen Mary's deep boom resounded over the city, tugs whistled fussily as they edged her into the dock, and there she was, enormous, majestic, the biggest ship in the world (American superlatives already came easily to me). We craned our necks to gaze up as she loomed above us, great expanses of startling black, and brilliant white topped with three huge, fat, red funnels topped with black again, and I thought with pride — she's as sensational as anything New York has to offer!

We were led aboard, up the spacious, thickly carpeted stairway displaying Queen Mary's personal standard, into the high-ceilinged first-class lounge, giving off a beige-pink effect with its maple panelling, grey-green carpeting and gilt decor.

Mr Hobson, our new boss, rose to meet us, a broad, tallish man with a paunch swollen with years of heavy eating and a farmer's round, red face. His grey hair was plastered over a high forehead. His hairy eyebrows twisted up at the ends and arched over a twinkle that made us smile with relief. He clasped my hand in a soft, but reassuringly firm grip — not the quick, formal handshake of the socialite. Then he introduced his wife, — "Mr and Mrs Williams, my dear," — an elegant lady in a long fur coat (was it mink?), who hovered behind her husband, her dark eyes in a round, pale face, darting from Alan to me. She said nothing, just smiled as we shook hands. She knows her place, I thought.

Another distinguished gentleman, tall and slim, came towards us and grasped our hands. Alan whispered, "Our new Ambassador to Caracas."

"Good of you to meet me," he exclaimed, determined to be met officially too. We hovered, caught between two rival VIPs, each demanding Alan's attention with, "Such a rough passage . . ."

and "I'll be going straight on . . ." Our travel section officer rescued us by whisking the Ambassador away and Alan escorted him to the door.

"Good luck in your new post, Sir," and then he darted back to Hobson, who was staring at the carpet, piqued.

The Hobsons were hurried off the ship. Their car was already alongside.

I turned to Mrs Hobson, "Let me know if I can help in any way," — a conventional and meaningless remark, since in the Service I had learnt that even to accompany her to their hotel would be considered unnecessary interference. Then they were gone.

"They seem pleasant, simple people," Alan remarked. "But time will tell."

Next morning Hobson signed the hand-over papers. He was now officially in charge. We could relax a bit, we thought, and see more of the children. Libet clung to my skirt whenever I was about to go out and would not let go. But it was not to be.

"The old boy is only interested in getting quickly into their flat. The hotel's noisy and they were thoroughly spoilt in Barcelona, their last post. I'm sick of hearing about it. Barcelona is everything that New York isn't. But their furniture and heavy luggage will take ages to arrive and then there's the redecorating." The flat should have been ready for them, I thought, resentfully. Now they'll have the same settling-in problems as we had.

Alan went on, "He refused to take over the out-of-office representational work, so we have to do the Dickens Fellowship Dinner tonight." "That's three engagements in one day," I cried, "Luncheon, a cocktail party and now this dinner! It's too much!" "It's a nuisance," Alan agreed, "But I don't really blame him. He's heard of too many C-Gs here collapsing. Anyway we'll sort it out eventually." I chain-smoked all day to keep going.

With no time to concoct a suitable speech, Alan took the one he had delivered the night before on British rearmament and civil defence, hardly appropriate for the Dickensians.

"I must think of something Dickensian to add," he said as we drove there.

At the dinner as Alan was being introduced, he reached wearily for his glass — a sip for courage. But it only contained iced water. Watching him grimace I stifled a laugh. He rose to his feet and began.

"Dickens was a publicist of the Christian humanitarian movement which is the background of the present British political thinking." He quoted Macaulay on 'Hard Times' — "one excessively touching, heart-rending passage and the rest," and Alan stressed the words 'sullen socialism'. The audience laughed. Then he laughed into our official line and gave facts and figures to prove that the Labour government, contrary to American belief, was doing the best for rearmament.

"Our defence expenditure now stands at 781 million . . ."

This talk of war and rearmament . . . I hated it and I knew Alan had no illusions that war solves anything. My thoughts wandered . . . our soldiers dying in Korea . . . are we right? Is it Russian aggression, not Korean? No mention of Russian troops, or advisers, not even rumours. And why should Koreans care about the UN or Allied resolutions? They're not in the UN. They're divided without their consent. And if they're fighting, not at Russia's instigation, but for their own beliefs, what of American foreign policy — this 'containment of Soviet military aggression'? What if there is no Soviet 'military aggression'? It doesn't make sense yet we're being drawn into it . . .

And my thoughts ran on remorselessly . . . Won't NATO force the Russians into rearmament? Create what we fear most, a powerfully armed Soviet State? I had covered the Russian front for Reuter's during the war and later I interpreted between the Soviet and British armies in Vienna; I knew something of the Soviets. And, I thought, General MacArthur is raring to get both at the Chinese and the Russians . . . My fists were clenched on the table. Applause cut me short. I joined in the clapping and telling myself that there was nothing I could do, I tried to attend to Alan's speech.

To my amazement the Dickensians were nodding approval as Alan flung facts and figures at them and the elderly ladies beamed at him.

"Lovely English voice," I heard, and "Such a handsome young

man!" Americans must be hardened speech-listeners, I thought. Alan concluded with Tiny Tim's "God bless us everyone," and sat down reaching again for his glass, but it still contained only iced water.

An old lady next to Alan asked him in a loud voice, "Dear boy, who are you? Why do you know so much about Britain?" Alan laughed. When the next speaker was in full flow, the same lady cried, "This is too long. Stop! Stop!" He went on unperturbed. Then she announced loudly, "The British are the finest people on earth." Suddenly I was relaxed, and I enjoyed the rest of the evening.

Hobson could not avoid functions given in his honour. At the first such dinner, he kept glancing round restlessly. Everyone knew everyone else except him. He insisted that I sit beside him. I understood, for we Foreign Service personnel had to feel our way before we gained the confidence we were supposed to exude.

Americans, greeting Hobson, could not resist exclaiming,

"Frank Evans was your predecessor. We loved him."

"Guess you're the new British Consul-General. Ah, Frank Evans did a wonderful job."

And again, "British C-G. Yes, we knew Frank Evans. What a man!"

Hobson's smile began to congeal. I whispered to Alan, "If anyone mentions Sir Francis again, he'll get violent," and Alan whispered back, "And if he mentions Barcelona again, I shall . . ." just as Hobson began "In Barcelona there was no hurry; one had time to think . . ." Alan turned away.

As course followed course, guests were encouraged to change places, but Hobson caught my arm and hissed, "Stay here!" As the wine flowed guests became more outspoken. Hobson's other neighbour began, "Why are the British afraid of antagonising the Communist Chinese?"

Before Hobson had time to reply, we heard a mutter, "What can you expect? They're commies themselves or damned close to it." Hobson raised bushy eyebrows. I whispered, "If you're not a MacCarthyite, you're a communist." I liked American outspokenness, their habit of pouring out feelings and thoughts and, if encouraged, relating their whole life-story between courses. It made dinners fascinating, but, after Spanish courtesy, Hobson obviously found American frankness disconcerting.

Mrs Hobson at the other end of the room smiled serenely, even when she happened to be sitting on her own. She had natural poise. But I could not help peering at her hair, beautifully set, but dyed mauve to match her dress, presumably a London fashion. Other ladies kept glancing surrepticiously at it too, possibly for future experiment.

We trailed after the Hobsons as we had trailed after the Evanses and soon I was again exhausted. Rooms were over-heated while outside it was freezing with a piercing wind. Rushing constantly in and out proved too much. I began to sniff, but I tried to ignore it. I must keep going.

After Hobson had met literally hundreds of people, in the Waldorf Astoria vestibule, he spied a familiar face. He rushed forward with relief and grasped the man's hand.

"How are you? Good to see you again." They nodded at each other and the man went on his way.

"Who was that?" Hobson turned to Alan, the social grin still glued to his face.

"Our consular doorman," Alan replied. Hobson snorted. "Too many people . . ." We did not dare laugh.

We gave a dinner in his honour. We had found a group of efficient, cheeful Irish women who took over the kitchen, which was a great help. They bustled about in shiny, black dresses with white lace aprons.

My cold was worse. I felt shivery but I was determined to make a special effort for this our first dinner party. I impressed on Alan that he must be witty and attentive to the ladies' comfort. No sitting back and letting things take their course. We had included the Canadian C-G and Mrs Green, and Lawrence Hunt, our consular legal adviser, a good friend, who wiggled cauliflower ears for the children's amusement.

We sat down to a polished table, the silver shining and candlelight reflected on the white, shiny flanks of our two Viennese porcelain horses, rearing up as centre-pieces. The ladies' jewels sparkled over their décolletages and evening gowns. Mrs Hobson, as guest of honour, sat on Alan's right.

"Your wife speaks perfect English, I can't believe she's Russian," she exclaimed. Several of the guests stared at me.

"She isn't," Alan hastened to reply. "She was brought up in England."

Then later, "She has no trace of an accent. It's unbelievable!" Alan frowned. No need to stress my ancestry in America where all things Russian were suspect, but Mrs Hobson kept repeating, "No-one could tell she isn't English." Alan was annoyed and I was surprised. So sophisticated in appearance yet so forthright, but I beamed at Alan significantly. He grinned back and gestured a maid to re-fill Mrs Hobson's glass.

The guests had second helpings of Mamoo's chicken and rice with lemon sauce as they listened to the Hobsons' talk of Spain till Lawrence Hunt suggested, "Shall we tell you about ourselves? Compare ourselves to you British?"

Someone observed, "The British conceal their wealth; we brag about ours."

"They're repressed, we're uninhibited," another added. "They know how to hold their booze, we don't." Everyone laughed. Americans, I knew, liked to receive and give praise but for Americans to criticise their countrymen was almost an un-American activity. Alan and I exchanged glances, but the Hobsons were leaning back, smiling, relaxed, enjoying our guests.

"You respect your intellectuals, we denigrate ours," they went on and someone whispered, "and drive them to suicide." Sudden silence. They had gone too far. Senator McCarthy and his witch-hunt were in everyone's mind. Several victims of the House Committee on Un-American Activities had committed suicide. Our guests fidgeted, avoiding each other's eyes. Alan quickly re-filled glasses. I nodded at Lawrence who cleared his throat,

"We shoot our Presidents . . ."

"No. Stop it!" his wife protested, and she explained to Mrs Hobson, "Two Puerto Ricans tried to assassinate President Truman." Others came in with more innocent remarks, the tension passed and the Hobsons plied our guests with questions. Americans were sensitive to criticism from outsiders, so the Greens and ourselves smiled but did not contribute comparisons. Finally I rose from the table and led them to the drawing-room for coffee and liquers.

At the end of the evening as the Hobsons left, Mrs Hobson suddenly gave me a friendly wink.

Next evening we found Hobson staring down at his engagement book, his face purple. "A communion breakfast . . . somewhere down Long Island. What next? It's preposterous!" and he went on mumbling, "I don't go to communion; I'm not a churchgoer and socialising over breakfast . . ." He was silent, then, "I shall tell them I'm a catholic."

"Better not, Sir," Alan interrupted hurriedly. "You'll have the catholics down on you like a swarm of locusts. Our C-G in San Francisco is careful never to admit he's an RC and he must know what he's about." Mr Hobson attended the communion breakfast.

A few days later, he announced, "I'm off to Washington to call on H.E" As Alan and I grinned his eyebrows shot up over that now familiar twinkle and he laughed, "Glad to see the back of me, eh?" We were. I was worn out. Impossible to say, 'I can't do so much', or 'I'm not going out tonight'. A feeling of urgency drove us. Back home there was rationing, heavy unemployment, and this talk of war . . . It was up to us, we felt, to do our best, and the war years had trained us to 'carry on' whatever . . . But my throat was very sore. I spoke in a hoarse whisper, spoonerisms poured out of me, a sure sign of exhaustion. Only that morning, to Alan's delight, I told Libet to read her 'Peetrix Buttock', and at a dinner party the night before I had argued that we must never, never use the 'bottom at'. I could carry on no longer.

"I'm taking action," I declared and retired to bed, to Alan's amusement.

As I curled up around a hot water bottle, I thought, Alan likes Hobson. They'll get along well together, and as I dozed off, I knew that I liked Mrs Hobson. So intelligent and that poise . . .

16

At last the Hobsons were installed in Beekman Place, they had taken over their representational work and we could settle into our own routine and lead a more normal existence.

We longed for exercise and fresh air and now we discovered a path running round a huge reservoir in Central Park, high above ground level and lined by tall trees and thick shrubs. I felt a surge of relief as we strode along it, above and away from the hurly-burly of the city, stretching our limbs and breathing deeply the cold, crisp air. On clear, sunny days we admired the intricate towers looming up behind the trees on the West side, edged sharply against the deep blue sky. But at other times driving rain struck at us, blotting out the landscape, turning to sleet, then snow, while a biting wind pierced our thick coats. Exhilerated, snow dripping down our faces, we trudged on.

We were now able to begin regular entertaining at home. Our flat was well scrubbed and polished for I had found a cleaner. Ruby came from Harlem. She was very dark, all bones, with drooping, heavy eyelids and a drooping, sullen mouth. But when Lawrence ran in, Red Indian feathers askew over one eye, and she burst out laughing, I saw she was very young, vulnerable and attractive in an exotic way. The children immediately scrambled on to her lap, and stared intrigued by her startling white teeth. We had never met a black person before and I had mixed feelings about her.

Occasionally Ruby disappeared for days on end and only sighed in explanation. When I phoned the Harlem clergyman, who had recommended her, he explained, "In Harlem they get the 'blues' and just sit there endlessly, and stare. So many of them have these spells; their life is hard." I had thought of the Negroes in Harlem as dangerous and primitive not as individuals with their own personality, but now here was Ruby suffering. It was disturbing — that drooping mouth ... I was glad the children hugged and kissed her, though I could not have done so; that dark skin ... but with the children she always laughed and joked. However, in spite of her absences Ruby kept the flat clean, the furniture and silver shining and I was satisfied.

Our cocktail parties went well. We could accommodate any number; I had learnt that guests preferred to be squashed up against each other. They rushed in, talking volubly, devoured canapés and devilled eggs, scattered ash over the Turkish carpet, made a fearful noise and finished off bottles of sherry and whisky. Then once they had met a few VIPs and displayed the latest fashion in suits and exotic hats, out they rushed and others took their place.

"Is all this really worth the government's money?" I asked Alan. I never saw any of the guests long enough to have any kind of sensible conversation. Then at a party in a Japanese home, to which I went reluctantly, as I shook hands with the smiling, welcoming hosts and watched intrigued as the Japanese guests bowed low to each other, the bitterness of the war slipped away and I no longer wanted either to tell or to listen to stories of Japanese atrocities. I had learnt the value of personal contact.

Our dinners were not going with the swing of the first. The five courses were well-planned, I thought, the table shone, candles threw intimate mysterious shadows over our elegant guests, and we relaxed. That was the trouble. Guests reacted accordingly and relaxed too, and the sparkle was missing.

"We've got to bestir ourselves," I told Alan. "It's the hosts who give a party zest. We must put our upmost into every occasion or the dinners will fall flat." It was taxing but it had to be done.

I could now devote more time to my family. I still worried about what they might say and how Alan would react. My sister Natasha, who came occasionally for week-ends, once remarked, "Senator McCarthy's doing a fine job, hunting down all these communists. They're everywhere; the State Department's riddled with Soviet agents." Alan grinned at her, sitting, staring at him with startling blue eyes, head held cheekily sideways, her slim arms round our plump Libet on her lap, and he merely raised his eyebrows. But when she announced, "Negroes are really happier as slaves," he exclaimed. "You're becoming a fine, old crusted southerner!"

Mamoo interrupted. Placing her hands on Natashenka's shoulders, she began, "Natashenka, listen! My nurse in Russia told me how your great-grandfather," she searched for an acceptable phrase, "'took care' of his women serfs, and how she escaped him only because she was appallingly ugly!" For once Natasha was speechless and Alan laughed.

When later I exclaimed, "How can Natasha be so intolerant?" Alan was amused. "She wouldn't hurt a fly, let alone a Negro or a communist," and I had to admit to myself that a few years ago I too held such views.

The Nebolsines, two blocks away, often dropped in and invariably started arguing. Once I remarked that 'As communists seek to increase material welfare here on earth, Christianity, which emphasises the afterlife, must appear to them as a religion of defeat.'

Kapa and Katia exploded. Kapa shouted, "Nonsense! Communism impedes progress. They're inhuman! All they want is power."

Katia outshouted him, "But it's Christianity that ought to work for people's good. Christianity is goodness and communism is evil!"

While Xana shouted, "What Aunty Masha says is a truism!" Kapa and Katia together turned on her, "Nonsense!" Alan laughed loudly and murmoured 'Nebolsinery!' a term that covered that family's eccentricities. I ceased to worry about my family's views as evidently they did not distress Alan.

And now we had time to visit Ashlyn and Mary Bagster-Collins, distant relations of friends in the UK, who lived in the wooded countryside outside New York. This was our first visit to an American home.

We walked into a room buzzing with the talk and laughter of their neighbours. Both men and women were informally dressed but they were as well-groomed as any New Yorker. All held tumblers, their faces glowed, and not only from the big log fire about which they were gathered. The room was warm and welcoming with comfortable armchairs upholstered in flowered patterns. The guests beamed at us. Mary, a southerner, with a pale, oval face and friendly dark eyes, and Ashlyn, sharp-nosed and ruddy-faced, kissed us, greeting us as relations, and made us feel at ease.

I was intrigued by the reversal of family roles. It was Ashlyn who grilled two enormous steaks over a charcoal fire while we women, including Mary, continued chatting over cocktails. Then it was the husbands who passed round the food and when it was finished collected the plates, and Ashlyn stacked up the dishwasher.

"What about a walk?" Alan suggested. Outside the untrampled snow was enticing and the twisted bare branches of the old trees looked intriguing. Mary glanced out of the window and shivered while the other women were shocked into silence. Alan did not repeat his suggestion. I was sorry to leave this cheeful company. They enjoy themselves, I thought, and make themselves so comfortable. Perhaps we are too hard on ourselves.

On the train back I was thoughtful. "I'm impressed. Here the women do the talking and the men the house-work."

Alan protested, "Mary no doubt works pretty hard behind the scene." Alan could not even boil an egg, but perhaps, on the whole since I was used to it, I preferred it so.

Through Katia I met a Mrs McCullough, a wealthy New Yorker who arranged meetings for her friends to listen to Negro educationalists. "She believes that once the Negroes are educated they will be able to help themselves," Katia explained. Here was a different attitude to the one I had so far encountered. These New Yorkers cared about the Negroes. But did I? Without having given it much thought I took it for granted that whites were superior and that blacks did not have our brains. But I had had a convent education and deep down I knew that 'all men are equal and brothers'. Not knowing what to think I accompanied Katia to a meeting.

Mrs McCullough, tall and angular, smiled at us as she shepherded the stream of women into her drawing-room lined with book-shelves, and with magazines strewn over the tables. She allowed her guests to chatter over an excellent buffet luncheon of cold salmon, various salads and chocolate mousses with fresh cream. She kept us standing so that we ate quickly and hurried into arm-chairs with our coffee. Then she introduced a Negro whom she called 'professor'. He peered at us through thick glasses. He was well-dressed, his white cuffs and shirt collar were spotless. In fact he was smart and had he been white I would have classed him as a gentleman. He spoke well, as well as any of my Oxford tutors. I was amazed. He told us of the work the university was doing and of the financial difficulties they were encountering because students could not pay for their fees. When he finished the ladies were expected to bring out their cheque books and under Mrs. McCullough's sterm eye they wrote out fat cheques.

As I left I found myself in the lift with the black professor and I asked him how many students he had at his university. As I walked out into the street, I turned to him for his answer. He wasn't there. I stood there, the doorman in his smart uniform watching me, and I was angry. I had after all talked to him in a friendly manner. But he had slipped away without saying good-bye.

When I later mentioned this to Mrs McCullough, she sighed, "My dear, he wouldn't want to embarrass you, for you to be seen speaking to a Negro in public." I felt ashamed and humiliated. While I was being condescending, yes, I had to admit it, he was considering my feelings. He had shown himself my superior. But it was all wrong. I admitted to myself sadly that I was bigotted and prejudiced but what about the Americans' pretensions to 'equality for all in our country and for all in the world'! I decided to attend further meetings.

I began to take Patricia Dunlop, the wife of the New Zealand Vice-Consul with me. She was also 'foreign' — a South African by birth. When we walked in together, Mrs McCullough, outspoken as usual, announced.

"Mrs Williams and Mrs Dunlop represent Britain and New Zealand. Mrs Williams is Russian and Mrs Dunlop, South African. The conversation ceased; the ladies glared at me and the Negroes at Patricia. We sat hurriedly down at the back.

Mrs McCullough was a staunch Democrat and so it happened

that it was Katia, with her extreme conservative views, who unwittingly introduced us into Democratic circles. At one of her parties Mrs McCullough took Alan's arm and announced in her booming voice, "This is the . . . the . . . the British government."

Alan bowed. Unembarrassed she led him round fielding the verbal attacks launched at him.

"That Attlee of yours is lasting overlong," a guest exclaimed, "If only Churchill was back as Prime Minister we could work together."

"Prime Minister Attlee and President Truman get on very well," Mrs McCullough responded on Alan's behalf. "Anyway, Churchill's a bit long in the tooth — our age, you know, dear."

"You need a McCarthy to clear up Britain," another guest announced, and again she answered, "No honey, I've no use for McCarthy. Ours are free countries and we all have the right to speak our thoughts." Alan smiled, delighted. Although her wealth protected Mrs McCullough, it needed courage to speak out against McCarthy, even in her own home.

At dinner, Mrs McCullough mentioned the remark about McCarthy to her husband, a neatly-dressed, white-haired gentleman in his nineties. He remarked, "It's all a phase. McCarthys come and go. We Americans tend to go to extremes. But you need not worry about politics. We're now in for a mighty basket-ball scandal." and he chuckled.

Back home, Alan said, "I'm glad we've met them; they're true American liberals."

At a later meeting, as Patricia and I arrived, a white-faced Mrs McCullough was being carried out under a blanket on a stretcher. We hurried over. She raised herself on an elbow, "Take no notice, my dears. Go along," and she waved a long arm. "Attend the meeting. I'm only having a little heart-attack." She disappeared, still waving, into an ambulance. We attended the meeting. We would not let Mrs McCullough down, and soon she was back again smiling as usual.

Another Democratic friend, from the war years, whom we were now able to contact, was in deep trouble. Over tea he told us,

"I've been black-listed, banned from government employment." Stan was a lawyer, well-built, with an open, candid face. It was shocking to imagine him justifying deeply-held feelings and beliefs in public, at open hearings.

He explained rather pompously, "They got me because, in their so-called 'loyalty court', I mainained that every citizen has a right to advocate the overthrow of the US government by force." We must have looked startled for he explained, "You see. That's it. It's incredible to you too. But our Constitution allows everyone to say whatever they like. Free speech. It's important to uphold this right, especially just now with all the witch-hunting going on. I stressed, of course, that no-one has the right in any way to implement such sentiments, only to advocate them." He sighed and drew his hand across his brow. Then he went on, "But even though Judge Holman of the Supreme Court declared my stand to be correct and constitutional, that did not affect the decision against me." The reviewing board had quashed all charges against him of being a communist but they would not agree that every American has the right to advocate the overthrow of the American government, and he lost his job.

"Perhaps our 'Incitement to Mutiny' act would be unconstitutional here," Alan wondered. "It's an infringement of free speech." Stan sat up, eager for argument, and when he left he was smiling, head high. Americans are amazingly resilient, I thought. As he was leaving he turned back and said, "I hope I won't be doing you any harm by calling on you." Alan shook his head.

17

The crisp air of New York's spring, the burning sun, the quickened tempo of the city drove thoughts and feelings to extremes.

March 1st. St David's Day. The American-Welsh gathered to celebrate. Though we were members of St David's Society, Alan being Welsh by parentage and I by affiliation, I was not looking forward to the banquet. I shared the Englishman's condescension towards the Welsh — strange people, mostly working-class, and of minor interest.

In the Waldorf Astoria we walked straight into spring. Daffodils, their yellow trumpets still moist and fresh, covered the white tablecloths, and daffodils overflowed huge urns on the high table. Welsh spring had that very morning been flown into New York. Guests hesitated in the doorways, delighted at the scene. As we took our places at small, round tables, the women's spring gowns of pink, yellow, green and blue blended with the flowers.

A ruddy-faced little man, with a halo of stiff white hair, stood poised before the dais, arms raised to catch the company's attention and to demand silence. He signalled and guests burst into song. Leading the singing in a penetrating tenor, the little Welshman threaded his way between tables, gesturing to bring out here a man's deep bass, there a woman's clear soprano. Hymns followed native laments, the voices rich and tuneful with that tiniest vibrato reminding me of Russian singing, so sensitive, so true, displaying perfect judgement. The hall throbbed with melody and I revelled in the sound. Alan and I were moved to join in, though our voices were fortunately drowned by the powerful singing. We read the words from the programme, 'Calon Lân' (Pure Heart). And as course followed course, guests downed their food between verses, raising their glasses to cries of 'Iechyd Da' (Your Health).

The President called for silence and introduced the VIPs. 'The Deputy Consul-General'. Alan rose to take a bow while the guests clapped. Then the President called out, 'Mrs Wiliams'. As usual I was taken unawares. I felt flustered as I got to my feet — all those hundreds of now silent guests staring at me. I clung to the table and leant heavily over it, head lowered, thus presenting its crown to those in front and extensive hind-quarters to those behind. Resuming my seat, red in the face, I whispered to Alan, "Why do I always do something silly?"

He laughed and whispered back, "Nice broad bit of black taffeta anyway . . ."

The President presented a cup to the Joneses, with the largest number of representatives present. I raised my glass to a Mr Jones beside me, 'Iechyd Da'. Together we all sang a final 'Hen Wlad fy Nhadau' (Lord of My Fathers).

I was smiling as we left, my arm in Alan's, the sound of singing in my head, glad to be a Williams and all regret at having shed a distinguished Russian name forgotten. I had slipped lightly and painlessly out of my prejudice against the Welsh and the so-called working classes. New York had done the trick. I now felt part of this Welsh throng. I belonged.

Then came St Patrick's Day. We British were never included in the celebrations, but for Mary's sake we watched the parade. It was a monster show. The crowd lining Fifth Avenue stretched from 44th Street, for three and a half miles and was so dense we could only push Mary and the children to the barrier at the point where the parade ended.

It was in full flow when we arrived and from the spring daffodils of St David we stepped into the emerald green of St Patrick. Green tunics, green chest-bands, green tam o' shanters flashed past in an endless stream. School-children with excited faces marched to the rhythmic beat of drums, amidst the sparkle of bugles and trumpets, and to the clip-clop of horses' hooves. Bands of kilted girls swung past with bagpipes — a colourful sight but like America itself, it was overwhelming. There was too much to take in and the noise was deafening.

Suddenly a huge banner loomed up before us, 'England get out of Ireland'. The crowd clapped with enthusiasm. I was taken aback. That banner was aimed at us. The Irish were proclaiming hatred of us and the crowd approved and cheered.

"They don't hesitate to use us when they need us," Alan grumbled. "I gave the two Irish vice-consuls lunch yesterday. They wanted to consult me." I felt deflated, and for some reason cheated. Did we really deserve this? Right was surely on our side. Of course we all make mistakes, but generally speaking ... Mary was staring at me anxiously. Quickly I smiled back. No need to spoil her day. Together we scanned the faces of the mounted police for her young man, but their number was too dense. Some faces were black. Black Irish?

On they marched, friendly societies, school after school, but my thoughts were in a turmoil. It was humiliating to inspire such enmity.

The Knights of Columbus were marching past, their blue, green and white cloaks billowing out over frock coats, feathers waving aloft from cocked hats and drawn swords sparkling in the sunlight. I had to laugh, grown men dressed up so fantastically. It did not occur to me that our busbies probably looked just as ridiculous to foreigners. Alan remarked, "It's better than military uniforms."

We returned home for lunch and then for tea but the paraders marched on in their thousands.

"You can judge the size of the Irish vote," Alan murmured and I sighed.

For the first time we saw Drum-Majorettes, in the shortest white tunics tinged with silver, exposing bare thighs, and fancy boots, white gauntlets and hussars' helmets with silver plumes.

"I don't like it," I whispered as they strutted past, young faces solemn, swinging their hips provocatively and twirling silver knobbed batons.

"They're great!" Alan grinned, "though possibly more suited to the Follies."

"They're too young. Why make girls expose their thighs? There's no joy in it either. They're not smiling. It's just to please the males. It's sad." But Alan went on grinning.

Next morning we read that ninety thousand people had paraded, watched by two million. Alan wondered who had done the counting and I wondered, did all the two million and ninety-thousand hate us? Were we that wrong over Ireland? Surely the government knows best ... The Welsh had given me one jolt, now the Irish another. I needed to think it all out.

In Central Park trees were already bursting into leaf. From the office window the huge, brilliant green oblong stood out in the middle of grey Manhattan and green spots kept appearing here and there amongst the mass of concrete. The air was so clear that we could see twenty-five miles away. Alan's field-glasses were permanently to hand on his desk.

The feeling that spring was here drew us to the park but the playground was too crowded and the paths were dangerous with hard baseballs flying past. Alan decided to explore higher up and to take a picnic tea. I was glad to get away from disturbing thoughts. The scenery was wild with huge granite rocks and trees weeping into little lakes. The children ran and shouted freely. The few people about were dark-skinned. We found an isolated spot beside a pool and lay back in the grass, admiring our children. Libet squatted on a rock in the sunshine, rocking her large pink Easter bunny. Lawrence flung himself off rocks and fell laughing into the grass. We opened the picnic basket and started on the sandwiches.

Suddenly I noticed a black face peering from behind a rock. I turned round and saw another. Then another and another. Dark figures surrounded us. They crept up, closing in on us from behind trees and bushes. I could not believe it, on this wonderful sunny day.

I jumped up. "Alan!"

"Yes. Let's go." He was on his feet. Quickly, without looking round, we stuffed everything into the basket, seized the children's hands and hurried away. I wanted to run. The youths might have knives. Such hard, threatening faces. But Alan held me back.

Lawrence cried out, "Mummy! It hurts." I was squeezing his hand. I tried to smile back. I did not want to frighten him. At last we were back with the crowds on the paths and we slowed down and walked home in silence, not daring to say anything in front of the children.

As we entered the flat Mamoo came running up. "Thank

goodness you're home."

"What's up?" I asked.

"Children in the park. I heard screams. I hurried along. A group of boys — about twelve years old, were all round a little fellow on the ground, pulling his legs, tearing him apart, and he was screaming. It was horrible!"

"Were they black?"

"No, white. I shouted to them to stop and I tried to drag them off but they pushed me away and laughed and called me names. I was helpless so I ran back and found a policeman. He wouldn't let me return with him. He said he would manage better without me. And now I don't know whether the boy is all right."

"I expect he is. The police know best how to cope," Alan reassured her. "You're brave, Mamoo. We need an army of valiant persons like yourself to teach those hoodlums to behave decently." We were all still huddled together by the front door. Alan ushered us into the drawing-room. Children! And in gangs! I used to hear of hooligan children in the Soviet Union, but that was the result of a civil war and a revolution, and they were starving. But in the USA, the richest country in the world, supposedly civilised and constantly pointing the finger at the rest of the world. Do people here grudge the money? Don't they care? I was indignant. What about the 'fundamental decency and rightness of American life' I keep hearing about? These are American youngsters, black and white. To be afraid of children! I sat on the couch, staring at my clenched hands.

"Forget it," Alan told me. "You can't worry about the whole world."

"I can't help it. I knew everything before, I mean, I had neat, tidy ideas and I was convinced they were right. Now everything's turned upside down and I don't know what to think."

"Then don't think," and Alan laughed. "Anyway it's Easter to-morrow and that should cheer you up."

We were alone at supper that night, and I asked him, "Are you coming to the Midnight Service?"

"Yes. I love the singing, but how long will it be?"

"An hour, and then the Communion Service, another hour and a half."

"Will you stay for that?"

"Of course. I'll be taking Communion. I always do at Easter."

We were silent. I helped Alan to chops and vegetables. Then he went on, "Strange custom. 'This is my flesh . . . This is my blood . . .' Surely you Orthodox Christians believe in the physical transformation of the bread and wine into the actual body and blood of Christ. Transubstantiation. That makes it cannibalism."

"Alan, how can you? That's beastly." I stopped eating, but Alan sat there solid, untroubled, chewing slowly.

"But it is. Most ancient religions went in for human sacrifice. They devoured their king, their God."

"Don't!"

"But they did. In Christianity, the tradition has persisted, though the form has changed."

"And you read the Bible at night . . ."

"Why not? In parts it's beautiful and wise. But communion nevertheless is derived from cannibalism. You're eating your God."

"You make me sick," and to my horror I felt it. I put down my knife and fork. To eat one's God . . . I shuddered. Alan held out his plate for seconds.

"But you married me in church!" I was angry.

He laughed. "I'm merely stating facts." I stared down at the polished table."

We went to the midnight service. The little church was packed. At midnight the Golden Gates opened and the priest stood there in silver vestments, "Christos Voskrese!" (Christ is Risen), he cried, and the choir burst into song, lights blazed, chandeliers sparkled and the congregation lit candles from each other, lighting up radiant faces. The familiar, joyous melodies were comforting. The took me back to those childhood days, when we four sisters stood in church in white silk frocks, white ribbons in our hair, with Mamoo and Vania behind us. I was then enraptured by the flicker of hundreds of candles, the glitter of gold and silver. The church vibrated with the richness of the voices and I waited for the deacon's famous deep bass, reaching a crescendo, echoing through the church. He had to chant up to a high note and every year I trembled, praying he would reach it and every time he did. At the end of the service we kissed each other and all our friends three times, saying 'Christos Voskrese!' and replying 'Voistinu Voskrese! (Indeed He is Risen). When I kissed the Cross in the priest's hands, he gave me a hard-boiled egg dyed red with a little cross painted on it. Easter was the greatest day in our refugee lives.

Now I placed a candle before the Ikon of the Virgin, her dark face below its silver halo gazing down at me, at the same time making the Sign of the Cross. I prostrated myself before her, forehead on the floor. I was filled with deep, inner satisfaction. Then suddenly, unexpectedly the poet Tolstoy's poem flashed throgh my mind, 'The Russian people have an inexplicable deep urge to bow, and scrape, first before this tyrant, then before the other . . .' My thoughts in a whirl, I quickly rose and joined Alan, still standing where I had left him. Was it this urge, that I apparently also felt, to bow and to submit that had produced those Russian tyrants, Ivan the Terrible, Peter the Great and Stalin? I could no longer concentrate on the Service.

"Let's go home," I whispered to Alan. He raised his eyebrows but he took me by the arm and led me out. I had not taken Communion.

"Cheer up," he said. "It must be spring that's got into you. Relax."

18

"Look!" Alan waved the *New York Times* at me. "MacArthur's been sacked! That 'Prima Donna' General MacArthur!" He jumped up from the breakfast table. "Listen to this, 'General of the Army Douglas MacArthur has been relieved of his post of C-in-C American Forces in the Far East and C-in-C United Nations Forces in Korea.' About time too!" Alan left his breakfast and hurried off to the office. He wanted to assess American reactions.

I sat on. MacArthur sacked! He may be the victor of the Far East, I thought, and the great hero of the groups in Korea. They're ready to back him. But he's dangerous. He shouldn't flout the President's efforts to contain the war. He wants to 'smash the Chinese' with UN troops. As though that's possible. And our soldiers are involved . . . such heavy losses . . . young boys dying. For what? No, we mustn't fight China, nor, Heaven forbid, Russia. Thank God he's going.

I tuned in to 'News on the Hour every Hour' and discovered the whole nation in an uproar. The announcer reported,

"Richard Nixon demands the immediate reinstatement of the General . . ."

"Senator Joe McCarthy says President Truman was drunk when he gave the order . . ."

"Senator Martin has invited General MacArthur to return immediately and address a joint session of Congress."

I realised with dismay that the whole country was for the General and against President Truman.

At that night's cocktail party, there was only one topic — MacArthur's dismissal.

A guest shouted, "MacArthur's right. Bomb Manchuria, I say. Why should we stand for Chinese intervention and do nothing?" Remarks were flung out with an eye on us for we, British, they considered were responsible for MacArthur's downfall; it was we who wanted to end the Korean war.

"What's wrong with blockading China? We gotta crush these commies."

Alan tried to reply, "Do you really want to extend the war, send out more troops?" But he was interrupted.

"Why not use Formosa Chinese? Why should American boys do all the fighting? And if MacArthur disagrees with the government, why shouldn't he speak out?"

We sipped our whiskies and with difficulty continued to smile diplomatically, until finally we got the direct jab at Britain, "It's a socialist, communist conspiracy and Truman's fallen for it. What do you say?" This to Alan. So now we were a 'communist conspiracy'.

Alan began, "It's a United Nations affair . . ." but no-one listened. They want to fight China, I thought miserably. They're prepared to risk war with Russia. War! Always war!

Lawrence Hunt, our legal adviser, drew Alan aside, "They're gunning for Truman," and he lowered his voice. "MacArthur's brought it on himself with his insubordination, but he's out for the Presidency!"

We escaped early. Frightened, I clung to Alan's arm. Alan was to make a speech that evening so first he had to find out at the office Britain's official stance. Morrison, our Foreign Secretary, had spoken in the House. Alan glanced quickly through his speech.

"Here it is. 'Generals must submit to political control . . .' and thank God, Churchill has given his full concurrence. Americans only care what he thinks."

That night I lay awake, waiting for Alan's return. He was very tired when he came home,

"I told them we were sad but relieved and that 'Orders is orders'. They didn't like it."

The country became hysterical and finally Senator Jenner of Indiana declared that there was in the government "a secret coterie . . . directed by agents of the Soviet Union", and he proclaimed, "Our only choice is to impeach President Truman." The cry was taken up, 'Impeach the President!' I could not believe it. Gallup Poll reported 69% in favour of the General and 29% against. A taximan driving us exclaimed, "It's a disgrace, the

General being recalled. We should bomb Russia, teach them a lesson, and MacArthur should be given a triumphal parade in New York."

I kept worrying Alan, "Are they really going to impeach President Truman? What's going to happen?"

"I don't know. It all seems incredible. Truman's a brave man." Then Alan warned me, "They really are blaming us for the whole sad story. I wouldn't go shopping if I were you. In the office people complain about being treated roughly because of their English accents."

As we were leaving the office in the lunch hour, Alan warned Mr Hobson, "Irish pickets are out in greater numbers, Sir. It's an opportunity for them to rouse opinion against us."

"Nonsense," Mr Hobson protested. "They were here before because of Evans, an Ulsterman. I'm English. They have no reason to parade now." But to his dismay, for no one likes being picketted, a whole crowd was there, marching up and down with their placards. Someone shouted something incomprehensible. Mr Hobson snorted. Alan went on, "They're probably professional pickets, not Irish at all, paid by the hour. They don't look dangerous. Still, it's as well we have Joe."

Joe, a stocky policeman, Irish too, with a thick mop of dark unruly hair, was provided by the city to protect the office. He squatted on a stool by the entrance, gun at his belt, and was invaluable at making tea and sorting out raffle tickets for our bazaar. He had a habit, perhaps symbolic, of flicking first the tip of his nose and then his gun with his forefinger. He was well worth the pickets down below.

Alan was invited to view a film about to be released to the public on the atom bomb and civil defence. He found it depressing. "If someone lets off an air-raid alarm, the whole of New York will panic and more people will be killed in the rush for the shelters than by the bomb." We had already noticed exits out of New York set aside for use in the event of an air-raid. I turned away whenever we drove past them.

MacArthur was back home and New York was to welcome him with a monster ticker-tape parade. We first tried to watch the procession from the office windows but we were blinded by the paper blown across our windows and away over the buildings — great festoons of paper towels, ticker-tape rolls, toilet rolls, whirling around in fantastic shapes.

Above us people tore up telephone directories, wrapped the pieces in parcels and flung them out. As they fell the wind blew off the wrapping and the torn bits cascaded out like clusters of stars from a rocket. When the procession came back from 34th Street up Fifth Avenue on its way to the Waldorf Astoria, we decided to go down into the street. We stepped into a thunderous roar and what looked like a blinding snow-storm. New York had gone mad. Pressed up against the barrier, we peered, through the paper raining down on us, first at three cars crawling past, festooned with pressmen, photographers and radio experts, then a long line of black limousines, a military band, some veterans, and police on horseback. At last, when my head could hardly stand the increasing uproar, motor-cyclists appeared and behind them General MacArthur loomed, the focus of all the whirling paper. Tall, he stood erect in his car, a magnificent, an heroic figure, broad chest displaying rows of medals, head held high, cap low over his eyes, shading regular handsome features. What a man! A conqueror, an Emperor, a President! Women screamed and struggled forward. MacArthur saluted and smiled. I was enraptured, all thought of war forgotten.

He passed. There were shouts and bangs. The F.B.I. car, following him, had broken down. A whole posse of detectives poured out and had to run to keep up. Alan laughed. I frowned; he was unmoved. Then he pointed,

"Look! That's real efficiency for you!" Three huge water cars brought up the rear of the procession, spraying the whole width of the street, sweeping mounds of paper to the gutters. A small army of road-sweepers collected the paper and within a few minutes there was no trace of it. Incredibly practical, I had to admit, but what an anti-climax! And I was annoyed with Alan. He showed more interest in the water cars than in the General.

Next morning we looked for the usual figures in the press. Over two thousand tons of paper had been thrown out and the head of the Sanitation Department remarked that it would have been better had everyone remembered to tear up the telephone directories before throwing them out. Seven and a half million people had lined the streets.

We were to go down to Philadelphia to hear Churchill speak but he cancelled his trip.

"He's too cunning to get himself mixed up in this MacArthur squabble," Alan commented.

"How disappointing! I was looking forward to seeing him."

MacArthur addressed a joint session of Congress and the whole nation, according to the press, was moved to tears when he proclaimed himself, "an old soldier, who tried to do his duty as God gave him the light to see that duty," and he announced that he would now "just fade away!"

The uproar shifted from the streets into the Senate, where an enquiry into Far Eastern policy was held. We followed it anxiously, snatching newspapers from each other. The hearings took up six to eight pages daily. The Chiefs of Staff were at last given the opportunity to speak out, and bravely, we thought, they accused General MacArthur of having violated almost every basic rule of military strategy by driving to the Yalu river. The Head of the Air Force maintained that bombing Manchuria which MacArthur had threatened to do "would cripple the Air Force for years to come."

At parties guests were now uncertain what to think, and it was good to hear them wonder, "Do we want to fight China and possibly Russia too?"

"Well no, but on the other hand Truman . . . and Acheson, making up to the communists . . ." And they explained to us, "Acheson, the Secretary of State, is a friend of Alger Hiss, the communist, the traitor."

The Hiss case was one of Senator McCarthy's most sensational. We had followed Hiss' appearance before the Committee on Un-American Activities. He was a former senior State Department official who had held such high posts as Secretary of the UN San Francisco Conference and had accompanied Roosevelt to Yalta. Elegant, well-spoken, well-mannered, at his interrogation he was self-assured and relaxed. He joked, fielding and returning accusations which he evidently found ludicrous. He feels confident and safe, I had thought. Although he was convicted we believed that something was very wrong.

"He can't be guilty. I'm sure he's innocent. I know he's innocent," I kept repeating to Alan, who merely shrugged.

Presumably Acheson felt the same for he had pronounced the fatal words, "I do not intend to turn my back on Alger Hiss." We suspected that the Amercian urge to bring down those above them, the intellectuals, the cultured and what we would call the gentry, played a significant part in Hiss' conviction.

Later we saw Hiss on a newsreel, a slim, neat figure, his fine features drawn. Convicted, he was manacled to some criminal. I had never seen men manacled before and I found it shocking, as though they were animals. Hiss looked puzzled, withdrawn and very much alone, as he gazed over the heads of the police and the crowd of newsmen jostling him.

I pestered Alan, "What do you think will happen now?" He hesitated, "They're in a cleft stick. MacArthur's policies now appear to be too dangerous, but on the other hand, they don't want to agree with Truman. And the government don't have anyone with the personality and histrionic ability of MacArthur. Oratory and a good television presence have become so important." Then he laughed, "But MacArthur made a fatal mistake when he said he would 'just fade away'. It's become his theme song. He should have said his bit about 'an old soldier' — that was impressive — and stopped there. But you can't 'fade away' and at the same time rise to become President. And he shouldn't have used the word 'old'. He is too old — seventy three. I think they'll come out all right."

Finally at the enquiry General Bradley, the Chief of Staff, summed up the Generals' views: "MacArthur's policies would involve us in the wrong war at the wrong place and with the wrong enemy."

"It looks as though common sense has prevailed for once," Alan concluded and he sighed, "Truman's trouble is that his policies seem tame — to end aggression, safeguard against its renewal ... peace. That's not heroic stuff and has no popular appeal."

At a dinner at our friends the McCulloughs, we were astonished to hear our host asserting, "MacArthur should have been sacked long ago," and even more surprisingly his guests nodded approval. Democrats, I thought, and Alan asked, "Why don't the Democrats speak out and support Truman?"

"What? and disparage the popular hero? Much too cunning. Truman will weather the storm and then they'll rally round him," and Mr McCullough gave his usual chuckle. I remembered Vania's reaction when his son, Timur, said he wanted to go into politics, "You can't. Politics are dirty, dishonest." I was astounded and I thought gratefully that at least our politics are not dirty, or so I hoped.

Then one morning the papers did not carry a single mention of MacArthur, and at parties guests reverted to cheerful gossip. The storm had blown itself out. MacArthur had 'faded away'.

"Well, now we know," Alan announced.

"Know what?" I asked.

"To discount American emotionalism and trust to their common sense."

19

It was stiflingly hot and I felt drained of energy, but only a few more weeks till the end of June and the social season would be over. I dreamed of Long Island and of that top floor of Katia's country house, near the ocean with its cool breezes and the quiet I craved. She had offered it for the whole summer. But in New York, though the only sensible thing to do was to lie prone and sip cool drinks, people hurtled around fitting in all those last minute parties and that, for us, meant once again out every night. I braced myself to face it.

Our own final reception was for the Royal Commission on Capital Punishment who were in New York examining witnesses. It turned into an orgy.

The temperature soared to 97 degrees. We had no air-conditioning and I hesitated between opening the windows and letting in air but also blasts of heat, or closing them and shutting out both. In the end I kept them open, but my silk dress was already soggy and clinging to me even before the guests arrived.

One of our Irish maids announced the guests, mostly from the legal profession, whom we had never met before.

"Professor and Mrs Warner!" Alan hastened to greet them. The Professor, an American, was bear-leading the Commission. They must have walked across the park in the sun for both had red faces and beads of perspiration glistened on the Professor's balding head. His companion wore a wide-brimmed, straw hat and under it the white powder she used was caked all over her features, making her look like a clown. Alan went round introducing them, "Professor and Mrs Warner!" Suddenly she broke away and caught my sleeve.

"I would very much like to be Mrs Warner but actually I'm Mrs Cameron." Elizabeth Bowen!

"I'm so sorry," and I thought quickly, "Come and meet Lady Jebb." To meet our senior lady in New York was one way of making up for our gaffe. The two women studied each other coldly, the perspiring authoress and the cool, elegant socialite, both distinguished in their own sphere but with no common ground. I escaped.

In spite of the heat guests poured in, crowding the rooms and we sweltered.

Sir Ernest Gowers was heading the Commission. I longed to hear that it had decided against capital punsishment. I felt strongly that human life is sacred. I found him, tall, gaunt, in the melée and shouted above the hubbub, "What has the Commission decided? What do you think about it.?"

"I'm a civil servant," he shouted back. "I collect information. I don't have opinions," and he would say no more. It was disappointing.

As it became hotter, we became thirstier. Our guests gave up the sherry and downed tall glasses of whisky, getting very drunk. Mr O'Brien, the Mayor's assistant, a huge, well-paunched man, swayed dangerously. Sir Ernest turned from me to ask him how the Mayor's office coped with the overwhelming problems besetting New York. Mr O'Brien leant his vast bulk against Sir Ernest, stared through rimless glasses into his face and announced slowly and solemnly, "We don't, because we can't," and suddenly he shouted, "So you can have the bloody city." Sir Ernest backed away and Mrs O'Brien, a tiny, dark woman, pulled at her husband's jacket sleeve.

"Jim, you're drunk. Let go." He pushed her aside. "Jim, I insist!" She pulled him out on to the landing. But when the lift arrived, with a sudden gesture he pushed her into it, winked and the liftman and slammed the door. As the lift descended, he came back, holding out his glass and shouting, "Whisky!"

At that point Nadia shook· my arm. "Listen! That fellow's telling dirty stories," and she pointed to another member of the Mayor' staff. His hand was on the bare arm of the young wife of the Pakistani Vice-Consul, a Muslim woman, probably only recently out from under the veil. Her husband had seized the man's shoulder, but Alan quickly intervened.

"I'm terribly sorry. I do apologise, but please leave him to me."
He led the drunk, giggling, out into the lift, where the liftman
grabbed him. The Pakistani marched his wife off home.

I was by now used to the drunks, but I had never seen friends
drunk. Now I heard a thin tenor wailing, "Now let us stay and
bide awhile . . ." Lawrence Hunt, our legal adviser, puce, and eyes
bulging more than ever! Alan pushed him into the liftman's arms.
Eventually, helped by Wilfred Thomas, our Consul, he escorted
the remaining guests to the lift.

"Well, that's that," he grinned and we collapsed into arm-
chairs. "A bit of an orgy, but we've done our stuff for the season."
I could not help laughing though I wondered how much more of
this I could take.

We still had to face those last social events. A 'Combustion
Overseas Dinner' was mercifully in an air-conditioned room in the
Waldorf Astoria. The thrill of going out was over as far as I was
concerned; it had become an exhausting chore, but this was big
business, a change for me. A long table curved across the hall so
that the seated guests, the ladies in colorful gowns, formed a gay
letter 'C' for 'Combustion'. An amusing idea, and as I sat on the
inside of the 'C', my neighbours and I had to address each other
over our shoulders. I relaxed in the coolness and, head held
sideways, listened to a heavy, red-faced man with bushy eyebrows
on my right.

"I don't know anything about you Europeans. But I can tell you
what's going on in our Mid-West. We're having to burn our
wheat. Yes, Ma'am, burn it. Can't sell. No one will pay the price."

"But why don't you . . ." He raised a hand.

"Sure. Why don't we give it to the starving millions?" and he
swung a heavy arm towards the world outside, "The answer is —
we can't. We'd need transport and that's expensive, and who'd
pay? We're not a charitable institution."

I was shocked. We're rich nations, I thought, and what about
the UN? It was shameful. But I appreciated my neighbour's
frankness, admitting he knew nothing of Europe, whereas I was
too embarrassed to ask what 'Combustion' was.

With the next course my other neighbour, who turned out to
be a UN interpreter, started telling me the mistakes that creep

into records of speeches.

"A Pakistani delegate," he began, "talking of atrocities in Kashmir, said that Sikh soldiers raped 25,000 women. In the record it went down as 'six dollars'. We laughed over our shoulders and he went on, "Someone said of a speech by the Soviet representative, Vyshinsky, that it sounded like 'Satan rebuking sin'. That went into the record as 'Sounds like Sir Tan Rebuck Singh' and the obliging translator added in brackets 'India'" How refreshing, I thought, that Americans do not go in for our British small talk. The time passed quickly. Doors were flung open and in marched a stately chef, clad in white, bearing aloft an enormous silver platter on which an engine made of ice-cream puffed smoke out of its funnels. We cheered and clapped as it was placed before the chairman on the dais.

The chairman rose to speak. "We are all one large family . . ." A drunken guest, and there was always at least one at every dinner, scraped his chair in efforts to rise and muttered, "When can I get out of here . . . ?" No one took any notice. I seemed to be the only one to feel embarrassed.

Alan was billed to speak as 'H.M. Deputy Vice-Consul', several rungs down the ladder of promotion, but he was introduced as the 'British Embassy', a rapid reinstatement. He began, "I once told a politician, 'I hate speaking'. 'Do you?'" he said, "'I don't mind a bit. I hate listening.'" He had caught the company's attention and his speech on British policy was mercifully brief.

There was still a succession of cocktail parties. Americans thought nothing of travelling 100 miles to a party. Instructions were difficult to follow in the dark, and, once on the wrong 'Parkway', it was miles before we could drive off it. The Hobsons sometimes give us lifts. I found it nerve-racking but Alan was amused. Hobson was worse than him for punctuality. He perched on the edge of his seat, watch in hand. Both the Hobsons were inveterate back-seat drivers.

One hot, sticky night, Mrs Hobson began, "Ash! (the driver's name) go along 57th Street and on to the Parkway there."

Mrs. Hobson, "Look out for the sign. Steady on. Stop! Stop! You should turn right here, no left. This map is completely out of scale."

Mrs Hobson, "Henry, you're looking at it upside down." Ash, a former Canadian Mounted Policeman, remained imperturbable. He drove on while they made up their minds.

Mr Hobson, "Where's he going? We're completely lost. Is the man deaf. Ash, where are you going?"

"I'm going on to Route R5, Sir, as you instructed."

"It's wrong! We're on the wrong Parkway." And he peered into the darkness. Ash ignored all instructions and finally we stopped outside our destination.

"Seven minutes late," Mr Hobson grumbled, staring round at us accusingly.

Then suddenly newspaper headlines screamed 'British Diplomats Abscond' and 'Flight to Russia Feared'. Burgess and Maclean, senior officials of our Foreign Office had disappeared, an unprecedented event.

"That's going to mess up relations with America," Alan groaned. It was ridiculous to think they had gone to Russia, but all the same I felt alarmed.

"What's happened to them?" I asked.

Alan shook his head. "I've no idea."

At parties we were bombarded with questions, as guests crowded round, "Are they communists? Have they defected to Russia?"

"Of course not!" and I kept answering queries with, "I don't know any more than you." "They've probably been murdered," "No Foreign Service officer would defect," and "If they were communists they had but to leave the Service and go to Russia." I believed what I said but back home I pressed Alan,

"Don't you really know what's happened to them?"

"No, but I do know that they didn't take any papers with them and they gave no reason for anyone to believe they intended to go to Russia."

"They couldn't have done!" I was emphatic.

"They both drank heavily," Alan went on uncertainly.

"Burgess was had up for drunken driving in Washington. They might have been black-mailed. Some newspapers are suggesting that they were homosexuals, and that's illegal."

I was shaken

"Why weren't they sacked?"

"Influence somewhere, I suppose." It was mortifying. I criticised the Foreign Office for inefficiency and short-sightedness, but this was a betrayal of us all. I dreaded facing Americans, and Alan became gloomier as days went past without any news. In public I still maintained, "They may be drunks but not traitors. That's impossible."

Americans stopped laughing and chatting when they saw us and even friends looked strangely at us. The MacCarthyites had warned of a communist conspiracy, stemming from Britain and involving their own State Department and now this ... In Congress Acheson, the American Secretary of State, was attacked fiercely as though he were in some way connected. He refused to be influenced by hysteria and defended State Department officials so much that we wondered whether the right policies might be rejected in Congress merely because they were suggested by Acheson.

"A sorry state of affairs," Alan commented. "The State Department will hardly want to confide in us any more. What with Nun, Fuchs, May ..." He shook his head. "One can hardly blame them."

I dreaded going out, and I didn't dare think. Yet every day I had to say something. "They'll turn up. They're not traitors," I repeated but I hesitated more and more. There was no further news.

"Alan," I pleaded, "It can't be ... in our Service ..." I slept badly, tossed from side to side and kept thinking, if only we knew ...

The weather turned both damp and heavy. Both children went down with what Lawrence called 'erms'. Then I went down too. The children recovered quickly but I could not throw the fever off. It was all too much. There was no strength left in me. I lay seeing all those over-heated rooms, the screaming crowds, and all the time I had to sparkle, look my best, and with those questioning faces and the growing suspicion ... I shrank shivering into the hot, sticky sheets. The doctor shook his head.

"You're young, healthy. What's the matter?" He left a tonic.

The Libet peeped round the door, a smiling, dimpled face, "Better now, Mummy?"

"Yes," I heard a voice behind her. Alan stood in the doorway. "We're off to the country, this weekend. Doctor's orders." The ocean! Swimming! Sunbathing in the cool of the countryside! Yes, I felt better already.

20

Alan and I roasted, stretched out side by side on hot sand while a light breeze played over our arms and legs. Through half-closed lids we watched the ocean smiling, advancing in long silver crests, sparkling with myriads of diamond facets. The children's voices at its edge echoed across expanses of empty beach. Peace. I drew in a long, satisfying breath. McCarthyism, absconding diplomats, the heavy heat and damp of New York were far away.

Katia's grey, wooden colonial house stood, old and dignified, behind two heavy-branched, leafy trees. The family, bare-footed and in bathing suits, ate outside under a sun umbrella at a big wooden table. In the cool of the evening, blissfully unaware of the American convention of competing in fancy beach and country wear, we climbed into old, familiar summer clothes for at last we were 'off duty'. I never noticed the amazed and disapproving looks as I walked around in delapidated tennis shows, one big toe protruding.

The first weekend over, Alan drove back to New York, his face brown, his nose a resplendent scarlet. Mamoo went with him to keep house. She and I then took turns to stay, one in New York, the other in Bridgehampton, which was about 114 miles from the city, a drive of some three and a half hours.

During the first week the ocean swelled up. Waves turned into rollers and sped up the beach, crashing down, sucking foam and sand back in again. Impossible to bathe. The children splashed about in a shallow lake, commonly called the 'soup', which was cut off from the ocean by sand dunes. There I lounged and delighted in their round, beaming faces, bobbing in the water between the blown-up wings. The first day Lawrence kept crying, "Bye-bye water!" and running away, but in the 'soup' he felt safe.

The week passed quickly and Alan returned. He drove up, wiping his face, with wet patches on his shirt.

Alan and Libet

"Into the ocean!" he shouted. "I must cool off." On the beach he hurried towards the water, Libet scampering after him,

"Daddy! Daddy! Me too!"

He gathered her in his arms, stepped into the foam and began wading in.

"No, Alan, don't take her in," I pleaded. "Those breakers are too strong."

"Only up to my waist," he shouted back.

"Please Alan!"

"We're all right," Alan stood his ground as the rollers swept past, and Libet clutched him round the neck. I stood very still at the water's edge and watched them laughing, enveloped in spray. The waves swelled, grew bigger and bigger. Alan wasn't looking; he was shaking the water off his head, when suddenly the largest wave loomed up. It crashed into him. He staggered, lost his footing and went down, disappearing in the foam. Fists clenched I held my breath, waiting. He came up, but empty-handed. Libet! In those waves!

I felt sick. For a moment I could not move, then I rushed into the water. Alan was thrashing around feeling under it. I reached him and, braced against the water, buffeted, I stretched my arms out, searching under the waves as they rolled in and past. She could be carried out and so quickly. The foam was thick. We could not see through it. Seconds seemed endless. Then Alan disappeared under the water and he came up clasping Libet, a spluttering, laughing baby, tightly in his arms. We struggled out on to the beach.

Breathless, Alan exclaimed, "She was clutching my ankle but I didn't feel her at first."

I did not say anything. Though I was trembling I was too grateful that she was safe. We carried her back to Mary at the edge of the 'soup'.

Then we stood in silence and watched those breakers.

Alan turned to me, "You'd better learn to cope with the ocean, just in case . . ."

"I can't." I was frightened.

"Of course you can. It's easy." Alan the optimist. He enjoyed courting danger. I stared at those waves, their crests our height. I

Trying
to get into the Ocean

was tell and hefty, but they made me feel small and fragile. However, he was right. I should know how to handle them and if I refused, he would think I was angry, when all I felt was overwhelming relief. I crushed the fear mounting inside me and waded in.

"Wait till the crest of the wave is above you," Alan shouted. A large wave was advancing, its crest curled over above me.

"Dive!" I took a deep breath and flung myself low into it. Water hurled me around, I struggled for air, then up I rose and I was in still water, beyond the breakers, Alan beside me.

"See? It's easy." My heart was thumping, but I had managed it. It was good bobbing up and down in the clear, salty water, but I hastened to ask, "How do we get back?"

"You come in behind the wave. It breaks and throws you out and you run before the next one reaches you." I must do it at once, now, while my courage lasts, I thought. A big wave. I swam in behind it. It crashed and threw me out. I jumped up and ran. I was shivering but triumphant. I could manage the breakers, at least of this moderate size. I could enjoy the ocean. I laughed with Alan.

In the evening with the children in bed, Kapa and Mamoo took Alan and me on at bridge — the Nebolsine kind, with Arkadi playing Chopin, the touching passages eliciting from him a strange, toneless, melancholy humming, and everyone around us shouting at each other. I was amused as Alan waited for Arkadi to stop playing. Bridge required silence, but Arkadi, unable to hear himself, played on fortissimo. The piano was out of tune and several notes were missing. Alan winced at every discord.

"One heart," Kapa called.

"Two diamonds," from Alan. Mamoo was sitting, elbow on the table, head on her hand, and she murmoured, "That's lovely," and she began to hum too.

"We're waiting for you to call," Kapa said irritably.

"Two hearts." Mamoo was all attention.

"Don't be so sentimental," Katiousha shouted across to Arkadi. "Give us some Schubert for a change." Xana, draped over the piano, began singing in a thin little voice, 'Röslein, Röslein' Alan glanced appealingly at Katia, but she was smiling, serene. Her children were here, at home, safe, not like others, rushing up to town, away from their parents.

My "three diamonds" was hardly audible.

"Röslein rot . . ." Xana wailed.

"Small slam!" Kapa leant back, a smug grin on his face.

"You can't," Mamoo cried. "You haven't given me a chance to show my hand."

"Playing one, two, that's nonsense," Kapa replied. "Slam or nothing." How typical, I thought, the biggest, the best; small achievements don't count. Mamoo put down her hand. We leant forward.

"Rubbish!" Kappa exclaimed. "You've got nothing but rubbish. It's not worth playing," and he flung his hand down just as Arkadi struck a loud discord and we started. Alan threw his cards down in protest but it went unnoticed.

That night Alan remarked, "Russians obviously share the Asiatic enjoyment of noise for its own sake," and he pushed our bedroom window up and leant out. "I need silence." A strident cicada chorus flooded the room and as Alan frowned, I tried to control my giggling.

Then back to New York. It was stewing in damp heat. I opened doors and windows to create a draught. It was difficult to breathe; the heat pressed down and I sweated. Alan was better off in his office with the windows open, eight hundred feet in the air, well above the noise and stink of the street. I hurried over the shopping; outside hot gusts of air bounced off the cement pavements while the massive buildings blocked any breeze there might be.

In the evening as the temperature fell, Alan's friends dropped in, dressed in open-necked shirts and summer-weight slacks. Wives and children had left for the country or the sea and this bachelor life had become informal. They sipped iced beer while I prepared salads with ham and French bread for the evening meal. I refused to stand over a hot stove. Only five days to go and I would be in Bridgehampton. I pitied the Consulate staff, cooped up here all summer, without a sister on Long Island. I wondered how they managed to survive.

In Bridgehampton the house filled up with Russian guests. There was much arguement, laughter and shouting, but we went our own way, silent in their company, unable to talk of our adventures. I could just imagine my sisters remarking, 'You know Masha says the Mayor's assistant got so drunk . . .' Then headlines in the press, 'Mayor's assistant drunk at British official's party'. I was not silent by nature, but as Alan's wife I can't talk to anyone, I thought, not to Americans or my family, and I always have to be someone else, not myself. Then as I glanced at Alan, sturdy, placid, reassuring, I realised how lucky I was to have him. So many Foreign Service couples we knew were drifting apart. Yet abroad they had to appear friendly. How lonely each one of them must feel.

At the end of August Alan took a week's leave. I found him watching Kapa pruning a tree. Then he picked up some shears and started lopping off branches too. Not to be outdone Kapa chopped off more. Branches were falling rapidly. Katia ran out, pulling a sweater on, hair awry, not her usual elegant self.

"Enough!" She cried. Kapa drifted away but Alan kept looking round. Katia added quickly, "You can take these privets down." Alan rushed at them. I had not known of this passion for chopping. After the privets he cut down a wild cherry tree, then he pruned the wisteria.

"Why hack everything down?" Arkadi was strolling past. "It's more picturesque when it's overgrown."

"It will be the house next," Xana giggled.

Every day as soon as we returned from bathing, Alan hurried into the garden with Katia after him.

"You can trim the rhododendron," she hurriedly told him and she left him to it. A rose bush covering the front porch with sweet-scented yellow blooms then took his fancy. He pruned a bit here, then there, more and more, till suddenly, there was only the bare stem rising up beside the porch. Katia ran up and gazed sadly at it.

"It kept the porch roof shingles damp. Look, there's mildew here," Alan consoled her. Katia thought quickly, then announced,

"You can take that large privet, outside the kitchen door down." Alan tackled it, chopping, and hacking at the old stems, twenty feet tall, and at least five inches in diameter, till they were all down. Then he dug a hole round the enormous root of the tree stump. But that was all he could do. The root was too deep.

"Pity, but I can't shift that," he said.

At the moment a Prince Gagarin stopped beside the root. He was a regular visitor. (Royalty in Russia were Grand Dukes and Grand Duchesses; Prince was not a royal title and was inherited by all the children.) He was tall, held himself straight, his long thin nose lifted in disdain. He referred to Americans as 'uncouth savages' and as Alan's silence spoke loudly of disapproval, he deliberately went into Russian, which Alan did not understand, making his admiring audience laugh, and hoping Alan would think he was the subject of their mirth. Alan took an instant dislike to him.

"You won't get that out," the Prince said pointing to the root. "Much too heavy."

Alan contemplated it, and I realised it had become a challenge. He started filling the hole in with earth and shifting the root to make it ride up on top. He struggled with it all morning. The others lounged in deck-chairs in the shade of a big mulberry tree, sipping iced drinks.

"Come and join us," Kapa called. "Leave off. You've done enough. I've made zakuski," and he pointed to a low table laden with tempting platters. Alan shook his head.

After lunch he was at it again, filling in the earth, heaving on the enormous stump. In his faded khaki shorts, earth smeared

Myself with Libet and Lawrence

over his naked chest and back, sweat pouring down him, he was hardly an elegant figure. The Prince's nostrils flared as he ambled past. Alan ignored him. I hovered near-by, afraid he would strain himself. He poured in earth, hauled on the stump, grunted, sighed. Suddenly the stump began to rise, up and up it went, Alan breathed rapidly, hauling for all he was worth, and at last reached ground level. Then one last haul and Alan staggered back as it came out on top. He straightened up, grinning and trundled the stump away triumphantly on a wheel-barrow, right past the Prince, who stopped washing his car as he gaped at Alan's filthy but proudly straightened back.

On the last day of Alan's leave, the Pouschines arrived, Vavania bringing a young friend with him. There was talk of a hurricane approaching Miami, upsetting the weather all along the East coast. We all hurried down to the beach to watch the waves.

"Too dangerous to bathe," Vania remarked, but a local farmer's son went in. The waves were mountainous. At exactly the right moment, he sprang into the breaker and we saw his body shoot up twenty feet in front of the wave, just inside the water, and as the wave crashed down, it left him bobbing about in smooth water beyond. We watched him rise and fall, his body lean and firm, limbs straight, head held high — an impressive sight.

Vavania's friend ran down into the water to join him. No one realised he was not experienced. Vavania was a trained life-guard. Almost immediately the young man was knocked down, rolled, sucked back into the water, tossed, crushed by a breaker and carried out away from the beach. Ignoring Nadia's restraining hands, Vavania rushed in. He dived again and again till he reached his friend. Keeping at his side, he shouted, "Dive!" They disappeared. Then both reappeared. "Back! Run back! Quick, turn! Dive!" They disappeared again into the next wave. I wanted to look away, but I could not. Vania stood motionless at the water's edge. Nadia was kneading her dress. No one spoke. They came nearer and nearer, Vavania shouting instructions, the young man obeying, as they dived, ran back, turned, dived again, two slight figures, under the mighty threatening jaws of the ocean. "Now, run!" They scrambled out of the water. The young man was pale

My sister Katia's Bridgehampton house

and he was trembling. Vania flung him a towel. No one said anything.

It was cool now and autumn was in the air. We left the children for another week and drove at night back to New York. The air grew sultry. There was no wind. Suddenly a temendous flash lit up the countryside. Thunder crashed around us. Rain poured down. Impossible to see the sides of the road. Lightening, thunder, pouring rain. We splashed through deep puddles.

"Stop, Alan, stop!" I pleaded. He strained to see through the whirling windscreen wipers. But the car sped on past all the vans and cars pulled up at the sides of the road.

"Please, Alan, stop." Huge hail-stones struck the car. We were blinded. "I can't stand it." His expression was hard, determined as he rushed through the storm. Useless to plead, I realised. I fell silent, not daring to speak or move. Why must he always fight nature, I wondered. Then we outran the storm and drove on in silence. He must have a need to take risks, I thought, to face challenges. Perhaps all men do, but I'm a coward. I don't like risks and I don't like the hurricane season.

Back at the flat, Alan sighed, exclaiming, "That was good!" He was bronzed, smiling, no more shadows under his eyes. He went on "And you look fine."

"I am," I smiled back. "I'm ready for anything."

21

Labour Day was past.

"Back into black silk and silver fox furs," I sighed, "but I'll buy myself one of those frivolous veils with velvet bows. That'll be better than a hat in those over-heated rooms." And so we plunged into the autumn social whirl. I felt fit and ready for it, but we must keep healthy, I thought. We have to look festive and express constant delight. But it will be easier now after a year here; we'll be among people we have at least seen before and repeating some of the functions.

It began with the arrival of H.M.S. Superb.

"I hope to goodness it works out all right." Alan had organised the visit. "Drawing up the guest list was tricky; everyone expects to be invited."

I had never experienced a naval visit. "Why are they coming?" I asked.

"To show the flag and do a bit of propaganda for Britain. Uniforms are impressive and as the saying goes, everyone loves a sailor."

The Superb arrived. I was not involved in the official calls. "And you don't come to the dinners," Alan told me. "It's men only; no girls. The officers will be furious," and he laughed, "but American men are always trying to get away from their women-folk and it's them we have to please."

So my first contact with the navy was at the Hobsons' cocktail party held in their Beekman Place garden. The officers were to meet New York's VIPs, mostly elderly officials. It was still strictly duty for them.

The Hobsons remained at the garden entrance, "But you stay in the garden," they told us. Guests shook their hands, then joined us so it was we who were left to do the introductions and to entertain. "Very cunning," Alan remarked.

The Navy arrived. There was a flutter of excitement as they poured in, a mass of large straight-backed blue-uniformed men with gleaming brass buttons, hair plastered down and beaming, friendly faces. They dispersed. I knew none of the guests. The American Admiral, an imposing gold-braided figure was standing alone, and a young officer was also by himself. Eager to do my duty, I approached the officer. "Let me introduce you to someone. What's your name?" and I led him across to the Admiral.

"Yes. Yes, I know his name," the Admiral said, glaring at the red-faced youngster drawn up before him. "He's my aide."

I laughed with embarrassment. I should have recognised the American insignia, but the Admiral was not amused and turned away.

A strong wind forced us to retreat into the basement rooms where, under the low ceiling, the heat built up. Voices grew louder and the noise became deafening. Roars of naval laughter and exclamations of "I say, old boy . . ." resounded as glasses were refilled again and again. I threw out trivial remarks till I hoarse as I pushed my way through the throng with plates of food. Then I spotted Mrs Hobson, hair blue for the occasion, sitting alone on a couch. She beckoned.

"I'm recovering. Can't stand it any more," she whispered. I sat down beside her, stretching out aching legs. But only for a moment. Mr Hobson was suddenly there.

"What do you think you're doing?" he turned on his wife. I sprang up. "Mix! Entertain! That's what you're here for." Mrs Hobson winked at me and disappeared among the guests.

"Well, that went off all right," Alan was relieved as we drove home. "These were the high and mighty so it was a bit sticky."

Next morning as we drove to pick up the Admiral for a service in the Cathedral, Alan warned me, "Don't talk to him. It's his only chance to recoup and collect his thoughts. His speech went down fine last night, good and breezy, but he's got two more dinners."

"What did he say?"

"He went on about successful co-operation during the war and then stressed that as America's chief ally, they should consider our point of view too." Then Alan laughed, "When we rose solemnly to drink the toast to the President, a young man shouted 'Boo!' but no one took any notice. They don't seem to mind."

In the car, I smiled at the Admiral, impressive in his regalia, chest covered in medals, and then ignored him. He nodded and stared out of the window.

Next day Ruby and I scrubbed and polished the flat for our party, and I removed all the small objects. We had lost ashtrays and knick-knacks as guests took souvenirs.

About a hundred turned up, including the Admiral in a loud and cheerful mood with two Captains. Alan had included in the entertainments the crew of a merchant ship which had docked in New York. Her Captain, a hefty man with a heavy red face, in a crinkled uniform, but now of the Admiral's own party, grinned as he watched officers in their smart uniforms edge nervously away.

Alan had roped in every girl he knew or had heard of and whiskies in hand, the officers advanced on them. No need for introductions. In no time every girl had an officer leaning and leering over her. After the Admiral's party had left, officers and girls sat entwined on the couches whispering late into the evening. Alan glared at the clock and exclaimed, "It's getting late!" He stopped the drinks, but they sat on. At last he said firmly and loudly, "Come! It's time to go," and reluctantly they left.

Next a dance at the English Speaking Union. Couples had paired off by now. As those blue-coated young men and slender girls in wide skirts and off-the-shoulder gowns swung round the floor, the officers gazed into the girls' faces with that rapt, enchanted look that said they had never seen anything as ravishing before, and the girls responded, creeping closer into their arms. The American girls wound their arms round the officers' necks and the young men deposited little kisses on their hair. I understood why the Navy is never allowed to stay more than a few days ashore. Suddenly there was a great uproar and heads turned as Mr Hobson, the Admiral and the two Captains rolled in, flushed and laughing upproariously. "We need a drink," the Admiral cried. They had come from a businessmen's dinner and the Admiral's speech must have gone down well.

Alan whispered in his ear, "It's a TT show, Sir." The Admiral slapped him on the back and whole party collapsed into arm-chairs.

"Your health!" the Admiral roared raising his glass of lemonade to Alan.

The last event was a cocktail party for five hundred, a mixture of officials and girls, on board the Superb. The steel-gray deck with its guns and oddly-shaped objects covered in canvas was austere but officers were warm in their welcome and pressed drinks on their guests. A bitterly cold wind allowed the young men to lead their girls away for shelter. Alan and I, exploring the ship, kept stumbling over couples, close together, behind ammunition lockers or boat winches.

At sunset, the Marine Guard beat a smart retreat. As the guards' band in blue and red uniforms and white helmets marched past, to the Navy's embarrassment guests applauded and a woman exclaimed, "They're just wonderful! So cute!" As the flag was lowered to the haunting sound of a bugle, the whole company stood at attention, and women cried, "Lovely!" and "Divine!" Guests stayed on, late into the night. Evidently the visit had been successful.

Next day the Superb sailed back to Bermuda, leaving behind broken hearts and one rating, who was very sorry for himself.

"He'll lose a month's pay," Alan told me, "and shore leave, and he'll have to pay for his trip back by liner. I hope whatever he was doing was worth it!"

And for us it was back to the normal social round and to those cocktail parties that I dreaded. Soon Alan's back began to ache. Standing after long hours in the office was a strain. He lay in hot baths, snapping at me, "Oh, do stop fussing!"

Elections in Britain had brought Conservatives, with Churchill at their head, back to power. My feelings were mixed but Americans were triumphant.

"Now that Churchill's in, he'll do away with Socialism," a local politician exclaimed at a party. "No more health schemes and they'll denationalise the railways and mines."

I suggested, "But your veterans are cared for by the State and that's a kind of health scheme and with military service that covers practically all male adults." But what I said as irrelevant.

Though Americans, I thought, because of the expense, live under constant fear of falling ill, they have this obscure feeling that socialised medicine is immoral, un-American and an infringement of their liberty.

As party followed party I began again to find it more and more difficult to cope with airless rooms, crammed with people. I kept feeling giddy. I tried to stay on the edge of crowds but there I was always easy prey.

"And how come you are still with us?" I was cornered by a guest one evening, "How can you serve different governments with different policies? Isn't that disloyal?"

I took myself in hand. I knew the answer; I had heard Alan giving it.

"We serve the country, not a party, and foreign policy, the country's interests abroad, remains much the same."

My head was spinning and I steadied myself with a hand on an occasional table. A Congressman loomed up. "Now that Churchill's back, I can tell you what we really think of Britain. Your people don't work hard enough, business executives feel they get no reward for extra work and your working classes are keener on their rights than on their duties."

I stared hypnotised into his rimless glasses and began, "But . . ." That was as far as I got. There was no stopping him, though I wondered as I listened, perhaps management and workers have drifted too far apart, perhaps workers have no interest in working hard, but I couldn't admit all this. "We hope Churchill will infuse a spark of enthusiasm to produce the hard work necessary if you are to get out of the present crisis."

He was blurred and seemed to be swaying back and forth, and his voice came and went but with a great effort I managed to answer,

"That's not fair. We've achieved solvency. We've raised industrial production 50% and exports 70% above pre-war level." Hopeless at figures, I had learnt those by heart. "This means sacrifices. We have rationing in order to pay our way. One egg and eight pence of meat a week!"

He smiled at my earnestness. Then suddenly everything spun round and went grey. Alan was back beside me. I clutched his arm, and gasped, "I'm going to faint." He led me out, and I was all right once we were outside.

"How can they breathe in there?" I whispered miserably. "There's no air at all!"

"Breathe deeply, stand legs slightly apart, and change posture from time to time. It's what we were taught in the O.T.C."

I followed his advice. I took deep breaths, switched my weight from one leg to the other and avoided standing in one spot. It helped. I enjoyed arguing and countering criticism of Britain, but there was too much of everything. I was always trying to catch up with myself and already I felt so tired. And now the bazaar was at hand once more.

Mrs Hobson asked me to take charge of the Commonwealth Consulates' Booth, "Since you did such a splendid job last year, my dear," she added with a glint in her eye. I sighed but had to agree. This time I had my notes and Dorrie was experienced. We plunged into the preparations by day. As for the evenings, we had reached the banquet season.

First the Pilgrims. At least here we were seated and there was no crowding. We could savour the oysters on the half-shell with red sauce, the filet mignon with asparagus tips, mushrooms and parsley. We could lean back and sip coffee during the speeches, smoke and dream our own thoughts. The Bishop of York, one of the speakers, a small, neat figure with a gentle voice (he was a Londoner), startled me out of my dreams by announcing,

"The real reason for the Anglo-American partnership is that we both believe in God." I pondered over this and since his speech was more like a sermon, I wondered whether I should extinguish my cigarette. When he raised his voice to pronounce the words, 'God Almighty' the whole room applauded and they applauded with even greater gusto when he intoned the words 'Jesus Christ'. Strange people these Americans, I thought, but I could at least manage banquets better.

Next the English Speaking Union. One thousand five hundred guests were seated at small, round tables. On the dais we gazed with interest at a host of distinguished speakers, Lew Douglas, former American Ambassador in London, Paul Hofflamn, President Trumans' special envoy, and Lord Alexander of Tunis.

Excitement rippled through the room as each rose to speak. But they proved to be excessively dull, droning on, reading their texts with hardly a glance at their audience.

"We must work together for the common good . . ."

"Our friendship dates back from . . ." I yawned. It was disappointing especially as my neighbours at table, with little claim to fame, were invariably interesting.

At the St David's Society banquet, the elderly gentleman beside me, Mr Hopkins, boasted, "The Welsh in America lead in vision and imagination. There's nothing worth doing that a Welshmman has not done supremely well."

"What exactly have they done?" I asked.

"I'm a miner's son, and my seven brothers and I all made fortunes here. In Cleveland, Ohio, the airport is named after me. That's something for a miner's son," and as an after-thought, he added, "And then there's Thomas Jefferson." Then he launched into the usual Republican diatribe, that sounded like a nursery rhyme, "Truman is a crook, he's surrounded by crook's. Roosevelt was a crook. All the Roosevelt family had the same lust for power."

Alan protested, "But the country has been run by Roosevelt and Truman since 1932!"

"Of course they get re-elected. You don't shoot Santa Claus!"

And there were other events to be fitted in. A reception for our Admiral Andrewes, the new C-in-C America and West Indies, where I met the author, C. S. Forester. He pursued the Admiral round the room, plaguing him with questions.

"I'm writing about Nelson's funeral. Would the Navy object if I described how the boat bringing the coffin sprung a leak?" He monopolised the Admiral. I was impressed — that's the way to get details right, I thought. The Admiral was amused and answered good-naturedly.

At a pre-view of 'The Lady of the Lamp', at which I had to replace Alan, I took Nadia with me. In a hotel room a few rows of seats were arranged for the press. Anna Neagle, Florence Nightingale in the film, greeted us and gave us her lovely Hollywood smile. We sat just in front of her. Nadia was so moved she mopped her eyes throughout the film and gave occasional sobs, while I sniffed into my handkerchief. When it was over Anna Neagle was smiling delightedly all over her gentle face and she shook our hands with both hers.

All this time, though I hardly saw the children, I was conscious of little beings crawling around the flat, murmouring about three bears or the cow and her calf. Then there was a loud stamping of feet as 'Mummy' and 'Daddy' went for a walk in Alan's boots and my overshoes. Once I heard Mary shouting, "You're naughty. I won't read to you," and then Lawrence whispered to Libet, "I naughty, but I had 'scusses."

I started pains in my stomach. At night I was doubled up in bed. I tried to ignore them but the pace was gruelling. "I'm so tired," I complained to Alan. "It's all fascinating but I can't take it all in. I'm worn out, and now the bazaar is about to start." I had to be efficient, cheerful and see everyone through it.

At lunch Alan arrived with a case of champagne.

"We must all drink a glass," he said firmly. The cork struck the ceiling, froth spurted out of a bottle. Mamoo sighed, elbow on the table and head on her hand, in her favourite posture, "This is the only wine worth drinking," she murmured.

Mary held her nose. She wasn't used to wine. "It's horrible," she exclaimed. After just one glass, I could not stop talking, "Mary, you must have some more. Come, Mamoo, let's all have another glass . . ."

So with the aid of the daily dose of champagne for lunch, I sailed through the three days of the bazaar in a haze. We made over 3,000 dollars, even more than the previous year. When it was over, Alan produced the remnants of the champagne. I was shivering with exhaustion and the first mouthful went straight to my head. I climbed on to an empty packing case and to the astonishment of the 'Daughters', who stared up at the British Deputy Consul-General's wife perched high up there, I raised my glass and shouted, "Here's to us all!" and downed the contents in one.

22

"Your dress! It's hanging off you!" Alan exclaimed. "You've grown so thin!"

I nodded.

"What's the matter? I thought you were better."

I stroked my forehead. "I keep getting headaches and diarrhoea."

"You must see the doctor."

"I have. He can't make out what's wrong," and I hastened to add, "But don't worry; it's nothing serious."

In the mirror a tense, haggard face stared back at me. I dabbed powder under my eyes to hide dark shadows and I put rouge on my cheeks. At functions I tried to leave early but it wasn't easy. At a party as Alan was talking to an American colonel and his wife, I plucked his sleeve and whispered,

"I must go home. Stomach pains."

"Right." But he kept turning back as he and the Colonel joked, "Did you hear this one ..." Friends of his, I thought. I hate interrupting; I'm always doing it, but I must get home. When he finally tore himself away he asked, "Who in the hell was that?" He did not even know them!

I was angry. I did not think it funny. Nothing was funny any more, not even the Daughters of St George, the ancient ladies as they formed an arch, this year not with gladioli, but with sparkling, silver-tipped willow branches. I made the effort however and this time was ready with a short speech, "It is good of you to cherish the links between our two countries ..." But I was shivering, my face felt flushed and my heart beat fast. Back home I found I had a temperature.

I won't give in, I thought. I've been ill too often. Every night the fever returned and I shivered even in a fur jacket in the hot-house atmosphere of the houses. The doctor was baffled; his drugs were ineffective and I still kept losing weight. I smiled and talked mechanically. I kept telling Alan I was all right. He had enough to worry about; but after each event I hurried into bed.

One night I could not sleep. I wondered . . . losing weight so quickly . . . feeling so tired and these stomach pains. Could it be? No, I mustn't think. It's exhaustion, the strain. This isn't a nine to five job; it's my whole life. But Alan warned me. I have to share his job, be whatever he needs. And if others can do it, so can I. I tossed and turned.

Next morning the doctor took a long look at me as I sat clasping sweaty hands.

"I don't like it. We'll have to start tests. I've made appointments for you with three specialists and we'll find out what's wrong." And he went away repeating, "No, I don't like it." It frightened me.

Next day, I crept down a long, clinically white corridor, lined with cubicles. I glimpsed patients, stretched out, waiting to be examined. A nurse in spotless white told me to undress and lie down on the couch. Then she placed squares of white material on me, presumably to spare my modesty, but I blushed and stared miserably at the wall.

A woman broke the stillness, "My God! Oh, my God! Help me!"

The nurse peered into my cubicle and whispered, "She's not in pain. She thinks she has cancer, but she hasn't." The woman kept shouting, "Help me! Oh, my God!" and I kept repeating to myself, 'She hasn't got it.'

At last I was allowed to steal away and on to the next specialist. I was prodded, examined, X-rayed. I swallowed liquids, waited in cold-white corridors, and did whatever I was told. I felt helpless, a wretched carcass. I took no interest in what was being done and asked no questions. It was my body but my generation did not think about health, or the body, except to adorn it. Doctors were mysterious, frightening beings, swathed in white, who pronounced judgement and had to be obeyed. I shrank inside myself and submitted.

Back home Alan settled me on the couch and gave me a drink, a worried frown on his face.

"There must be a reason for your losing so much weight so it's better to find out."

"I'm all right," I smiled back.

One more day and at last it was over. I was told that we would hear the results after the Christmas holidays. As I walked out of the clinic a blizzard was raging outside and the cold struck me. I raised my face to it. Eight days of freedom — the Christmas break — without a single engagement. I stood and let the icy air seep through me. How good it felt.

Fifth Avenue was in chaos. Lights flashed, abandoned cars were strewn across the street, others skidded over the ice. Buses jerked to a halt every few yards. No hope of reaching home by bus or taxi, but how refreshing it would be to walk. There had been no time for strolls round the reservoir. Now I had forty blocks before me. The wind blew away the hospital smells. People scurried past, heads lowered, but mine was up as I strode along and murmured, "Eight days . . . all free . . . eight whole days . . ."

Ashlyn and Mary Bagster-Collins had been invited for supper, but with a fifty mile drive before them, they would never make it. Two hours later I entered our flat and there was Ashlyn, his sharp features already flushed, and Mary beaming, both with drinks in hand.

"I thought you'd never come," Mary cried as she kissed me.

"I walked. And how did you get here?"

She looked surprised, "We drove, as usual." These Americans, so tough where driving was concerned; snow, blizzards, nothing deterred them. We settled in arm-chairs before our big log fire, feet on the fender — the Bagster-Collinses were not official — and we sipped hot glühwein.

An hour later, Alan arrived. "I was on a bus," he explained, "and every time I decided I'd better get off and walk, it started up again. I'm sorry."

The blizzard struck at the windows but inside with the curtains drawn it was warm and cosy.

"Dinner's ready!" Mamoo called.

The glühwein had been strong. Ashlyn uttered a yelp, sprang into the centre of the room and flung himself into the charleston. We laughed as his serious face, with its long nose, and hair brushed severely back, he pranced around, elbows out, legs kicking out, one mad whirl. Mary jumped up, clapped, and stamped out the rhythm with the toe of her shoe. I sprang up too and seized his hands. We kicked, we bounced, we twirled, toes in, knees close, heels up. Faster and faster, panting, grinning, away with sickness, strain, tension. I'm young, silly, frivolous.

"But dinner's ready." Alan protested as he stared at us, astounded.

"O.K." I called back and Ashlyn and I charlstoned down the corridor and into the dining-room, where Mamoo began clapping and laughing too. We flopped into our chairs, exchanged con-spiratorial glances and tucked into juicy steaks. I was hungry.

When the Bagster-Collinses left, I fell into bed and slept deeply. Next morning the sun glistened over a snow-covered park. I had dreaded the family parties, the work involved, the noise, the trailing around, but at our Christmas dinner when the family crowded in, carrying exciting packages, and exclaiming, "Happy Christmas!" and "What a lovely day!" I realised that there was nothing to worry about. I was just a sister, an aunt, no one special and there was no act to put on and no strain. I kissed and welcomed them eagerly.

As packages were unwrapped and the family warmed up with drinks, the children flung themselves at Vania. "Come on, ton of bricks," and Vania bounced Libet up and down on his knees, higher and higher till she squealed with excitement, and Law-rence yelled, "Me! Now me!"

Vania was so hefty yet so gentle and so comforting. My sisters thought him lazy but with New Yorkers racing around, I found him restful. He rarely spoke, but when he did, others fell silent. He liked to hold forth on public affairs and then, sadly, I had to listen in silence, for like my sisters, Vania was very conservative. As school girls my sisters and I had argued so heatedly, they on the side of Charles 1, and I for Cromwell, that Mamoo forbade us to mention either. Vania would not understand my championing the under-dog. "Who am I to judge?" he often repeated. "What was good enough for my ancestors, is good enough for me." Strange, I thought, that with the same upbringing we should think so differently. We must all be born one way or the other.

The children, exhausted, nestled in Vania's arms, one on each knee. He ignored the creases they made in his good suit. He sang softly to them in his deep bass, "Chizhok! Chizhok! (Siskin! Siskin!) where've you been?"

At dinner I ate and drank too much but the diarrhoea had disappeared. The family shouted across the table.

Kapa: "Bigger slices, Alan. We have Russian appetites here!"

Arkadi: "Papa! You make so much noise no one can be heard."

The others: "And who's shouting now?"

Alan kept glancing at me but I was glad our young felt at home with us, and yes, we Russians must like the noise for it did not give me a headache.

After dinner we gathered round the radio for the King's speech. Our King was nothing to my nieces and nephews who were American, but Vania's authoritative, "Hush!" settled them down in silence.

The speech was obviously recorded, speeded up and the pauses and stutters cut out, but the effort the King was making came over regardless. There was an ominous hollow echo as he struggled on, "... we can offer to the world ... tolerance and understanding that runs like a golden thread through the great and diverse family of the British Commonwealth of Nations." His lung operation must have been serious. I longed to stop the broadcast, to shield the King, to say, "Never mind. Don't try any more. We understand." It was painful to listen and when it was over there was silence. Mamoo sighed and we avoided looking at each other till the children shouted, "Uncle Chocolate! More!" and the noise and chatter started up again.

That night Mamoo and I pored over the New Yorker Album that Alan had given me for Christmas.

"How vulgar!" I exclaimed, grinning over a mountainous lady in an art gallery gazing up at a Rubens fleshy nude and saying to her husband, 'Why Ted, you say the sweetest things.'

We turned the pages over eagerly and, watching, Alan was pleased to see me laughing.

Christmas was over but we still had four days of freedom.

"Spend the time with the children in the open air," Alan suggested.

In the park a teacher with a group of infants in front of the local club-house called to us, "Come and join us. All little ones are welcome. I'm here every day, whatever the weather. Bring them along."

I strolled about, snow crunching under my boots, watching twelve little children, tubby in their colourful snow-suits, prancing up and down, singing, 'Here we go loopy-loo ...' Libet brought a thin little girl, called Barbara, back to tea and Barbara invited the children to her birthday party.

"She's Jewish," Mary told me. "Her nanny said that our children would be the only non-Jews there. Did you mind? Barbara is only invited into Jewish homes but she has been here." How ridiculous, I thought, especially in a Jewish city like New York, and how hurtful.

The children went, and returned laden with presents.

"I'z only boy. I'z 'Farmer in the Dale'", Lawrence shouted. And Mary told us,

"The grandmother wanted to keep Libet. She's plump and she ate all the good things the grandmother prepared."

The eight days were over.

"Come to the office with me," Alan suggested. "The specialists' reports should be there." I bit my lip and my heart raced. In the office the envelope lay on Alan's desk. He sat down opened it. I waited, stiff against the wall.

"Nothing!" he exclaimed. "There's nothing wrong with you." We stared at each other. Alan looked down again and added glumly, "And it's going to cost the tax-payer more than somewhat. I hardly dare send these bills to the Embassy." Our medical bills all went to Washington for approval and reimbursement. "What a racket!"

So all I had needed was a rest. But I protested to Alan, "Why didn't the doctor order me to rest? How can I back out of functions laid on for us as guests of honour? I can't say 'So sorry I'm tired.'" I stared at the floor relieved, embarrassed and ashamed all at the same time. Our life's upside down, I thought. We have the luxuries, travel, banquets, meeting VIPs, but not the essentials, a regular life, fresh air, a routine, quiet, health.

Alan suddenly got up and pointed out of the window, "Look

at that!" I turned. The city, spread out sixty-four floors below us, lay in a deep blue shroud thrown over it by the heavy, ominous clouds massed above us, but beyond the clouds, the sun was out and it shed a glorious gold over the whole bay as far as the eye could see. We stood enthralled, close together, Alan's arm round my shoulders.

23

Churchill was passing through New York on his way to Washington. I longed to catch just a glimpse of him but, I grumbled to myself, we wives were never invited if we were not needed. He epitomised, for me, the war years in London with the bombs, defeats and final victory. He was very special. During an air-raid while bombs exploded in the distance and as I was listening on the radio to the Lord Mayor's Banquet, I heard Churchill, our Prime Minister, stammering, hissing through loose teeth, stumbling through his speech, obviously drunk.

"Come, quick!" I shouted to Mamoo and the others. "Churchill's drunk!" How we laughed! That the P.M. dared to get drunk during an air-raid infused us with courage. Sadly, after the war I blamed him for introducing the terms 'Iron Curtain' and 'Cold War', especially using the word 'war', thus dividing East from West. I believe that words can create situations. Nevertheless I would have liked to stand in the street with the children and see him pass. That, however, was out of the question; I might have been recognised.

"Well, I'm off," and Alan bent to kiss me. To greet his P.M. he was solemn in his short black jacket, striped trousers and heavy black overcoat. "I hope to goodness all runs according to plan." For weeks past the Consulate had been in a state of tension as messages flew between the P.M., the Ambassador Mr Hobson, the Mayor of New York, and the State Department, all pressing for changes of plan as they competed for more of Churchill's time.

"He's old," Alan went on. "Some say he's senile, while Americans are expecting miracles from him. They think he'll put Britain back on her pedestal. Anyway, bye for now."

"Good-bye." My voice was chilly and I sat on, still resentful. Then I thought, yes, Americans believe you have but to pin-point a problem, tackle it and it's solved. And everything is either black or white, but who is ever entirely right or entirely wrong? They're disappointed that the Conservatives have not done what they expected of them. The headline in the Herald Tribune stared up at me, 'Britain's recognition of Red China'. An emotional issue that Churchill will have to face, I thought. At a function I had been asked, 'How can Britain have anything to do with the brutes who are killing our boys in Korea?" I glanced down again at the paper. It called us 'pig-headed' over European Union. 'Federation works here ... obvious solution for Europe ... UK is part of Europe, so why does Churchill exclude Britain from the Union he believes in so strongly himself.' They still think the Commonwealth, and that is what he is promoting, smacks of colonialism. It struck me how deep was the antagonism that Churchill had to overcome. I read on, 'Why doesn't Churchill denationalise Britain?' 'Why is Britain bolstering up Russia's armed forces, selling her tin and rubber and buying coarse grain and timber from the Iron Curtain countries?' I sighed. However, I thought, if Churchill's not senile, with his prestige and great gift of oratory ...

I stayed at home that morning awaiting Alan's return.

"How did it all go?" I met him at the door, dragged his overcoat off him and propelled him on to the study couch. "Tell me everything, right from the start."

"Well, a cutter brought Churchill and all his merry men from the Queen Mary on to Brooklyn Pier." Alan lit a cigarette.

"Go on!" He was so slow.

"There he stood, a lone figure, his staff keeping their distance as with Royalty. He leant on a stick — squat, with stooping shoulders, bull neck thrust forward, a round heavy-jowled face under his homburg. A ludicrous sight in a way, but strangely impressive."

"Was he all right?"

"Oh yes, cheeks rosy and healthy. I chatted with Bomber Harris, his wife and daughter, and Mr Beauchamp, Sarah Churchill's second husband. Though sleet was falling and the wind was bitterly cold, Churchill beamed as the band struck up and the Guard of Honour froze at the salute. The papers had been saying that 'the welcome mat is definitely not out'. Well, it was and you should have heard the cheers. The police struggled to hold back hordes of reporters and press photographers, all making a wild rush towards him. Then, grinning all over his face and bushy eyebrows even higher than usual, Hobson led Churchill under shelter and introduced the local dignitaries. They bowed as they shook the great man's hand, and then he stepped forward for his first press conference. He won them over straight away by joking that he would be glad to answer any questions with explanations why he could not answer them. Quite a scene — New York greeting the great hero. An excellent start. Then the whole party drove off in a motorcade."

The streets would be empty as, for security reasons — the Consulate had received letters threatening Churchill's life — the route had not been announced, and the police would move on the few people who stopped to stare.

"No unpleasantness?"

"No. Everything went off fine, though a long line of Irish pickets shouted 'Boo!' and held placards 'No money from the USA' and 'Take your troops out of Ireland'. Churchill grinned, gave the V-sign and they grinned and gave the V-sign back. Must have been professional pickets, not Irish at all, and further along a group of green-coated elderly ladies cheered and waved. But it's a relief that they're all safely on their way." Then he laughed. "I almost did not get back. The police motorcyle escort swept us back into town. I wanted to catch a bus home on Fifth Avenue, but how to stop the motorcade?"

"What did you do?"

"I opened the car window, waved at the motorcyclists and yelled 'Stop!' The whole motorcade roared to a sudden halt and I got out. People in the street stared. Motorcades rushing past are nothing new, but they had never seen them drop off a passenger."

At lunch he teased Mary, "What about these Irish pickets, Mary?"

"They're mad," she retorted, her large blue eyes indignant, "and Americans at that."

"What about you, Margaret? You're Irish too." Margaret, thin and with quick movements, had replaced our slow-moving Ruby who had disappeared.

"I'm American and it's nothing to do with me." The two girls glared at each other.

"And talk of Irish cheek," Alan went on. "They asked us to contribute a dollar towards their picket line! How do you like that!"

Mary and Margaret had to laugh.

The P.M. came through again on his way to Ottawa. He was to have flown but the weather worsened and in the evening he decided to take the train. When Alan got home, late that night, he poured himself an extra strong swig of whisky. "It was pandemonium. Our travel section had to be alerted, new train reservations made, Churchill's staff, out on shopping sprees, had to be rounded up. They had to pack and be driven to the train, but the drivers who had gone off duty had first to be collected. Finally, by some miracle, everyone was accounted for and Hobson was able to escort Churchill on to the train."

Then Mr Eden, our new Foreign Secretary, descended on New York to receive an Honorary Degree at Columbia. He was considered to be the best-looking and most elegant diplomat in the world and an eloquent public speaker; I looked forward to him impressing New Yorkers. Alan was once more plunged into co-ordinating plans for the visit.

The invitation to the Convention included me and I was delighted. The hall was full. Chairs were packed solidly and in tight rows, but they were small and beside me Mr Green, the Canadian C-G, who was huge and fat, overflowed on to half mine. Perched on the other half, legs sideways, entangled in Alan's, I dug my heels into the floor to keep my balance. Alan kept whispering "You're pushing me off my chair," while I could only make faces back at him, as we were seated directly behind our boss, Sir Oliver Franks, our Ambassador.

Mr Eden sat on a chair, alone, facing the audience. He had had little sleep on the plane over. During the introductory speech, as the audience shifted in their seats to get a better view of him, lights from the television cameras were focussed hot on his face, and as the speaker droned on, slowly Eden's eyes closed, his mouth drooped open and he slept. We were helpless; we could not reach him though the whole of the USA was enjoying the spectacle of our Foreign Minister sleeping peacefully, with his mouth wide open, looking neither handsome nor impressive. And later we were told, they also saw us whispering and Alan and me pushing each other off those tiny chairs.

Eden woke in time for his speech. He sprang up, now both handsome and elegant, and without notes, delivered a brilliant defence of our foreign policy. "The purpose of our armed strength (in NATO) is to provide a dyke behind which the practice of freedom may grow . . . that is the most that material force can ever do, or should ever attempt to do, in a conflict of ideas." That was reassuring. "It is not in our minds to use the new strength which we are building up for any other purpose . . . We must never cease to make it clear that peace is our objective."

He's sincere, I thought, but again that nagging doubt. NATO — a dyke, but is a dyke necessary? Russia's no threat to us. Korea, Berlin, but Berlin is in the middle of East Germany, a Trojan horse and if the Russians wanted to attack us, they would have done so before NATO was set up and while we were still disarmed. I was not listening any more. Eastern Europe, it's tragic but no threat to us. It's a defensive cordon they've put up to protect themselves from us. But I wondered, am I competent to question official views? I don't know all the facts; Alan never mentions any secret goings-on. It's all so confusing.

I glanced up at Alan's profile and wondered what he was thinking. He's not a party man, though he leans towards Labour, but I, a Conservative voter harbouring what Americans would consider subversive, communist thoughts! I laughed to myself. But I may be wrong and I mustn't harm Alan or spoil his career. Better stop thinking. I leant up against him. The speech was over.

Coming out of the hall, the Pakistani Consul, a tall, dark man, greeted us, clasped Alan's hand and held on to it, as together they walked down the university steps, with me trailing embarrassed behind them. Alan, who as so reserved and self-conscious! Standing at the bottom of the steps, Mr Eden and Sir Oliver stared with raised eyebrows as these two tall, handsome men strolled past them hand in hand.

When we later discussed Eden's speech we decided that his was typical British oratory, but for Americans he packed too much into it. He raced through arguments whereas Americans like slow speech and repetition. They are lazy listeners. Also we noted that when speaking Alan must bear in mind that television lights and the hum of cameras distract the audience.

Then the P.M. was back once more in New York and in very good humour. He had addressed Congress hoping to re-establish the 'special relationship' between the USA and Britain. Next morning the New York Times wrote, 'Congress gave Prime Minister Churchill today a more affectionate reception than ever it has given in late years to the President of the United States himself.'

"The old man couldn't have asked for more!" Alan exclaimed.

The Office was galvanised into planning his stay and caring for his suite. Alan kept outwardly calm but I could feel the tension underneath. I kept the children out of his way. Every evening they made a habit of waiting for his return by the front door. They were now arguing there. Lawrence shouted at Libet.

"Fatty!"

And she protested, "I'm not fat. I'm just plump."

And he snapped back, "Dumpling!" At the moment I heard the whirr of the lift, "Mary!" I called, "Get them into the nursery and please keep them quiet. Just for a few days." She nodded. I had already warned my family to keep away. Alan came in.

"How's it all going?"

He shrugged and over the snack I had prepared he told me, "We can't decide whether Churchill should or should not drive to City Hall to call on the Mayor. Hobson keeps dithering. He's a mass of nerves. He keeps saying, 'The P.M. might fall ill. The weather forecast is rain and snow.' Then he wants to know what the Mayor thinks. And as Churchill has already had one ticker-tape parade he fears a second might be an anti-climax."

Then Alan was off again. I hardly saw him during the following days but I kept hoping that the parade would take place and I would at last see Churchill. However, before anything was decided, Lord Moran, Churchill's doctor, announced that Churchill had caught a cold and must not go out. New Yorkers were disappointed, according to the press, and so was I, very.

Churchill flew back home and Alan murmured, "Thank God

he's safely off our hands." But I had enjoyed the whiff of greatness in the air.

Alan was left to deal with Churchill's fan mail.

"What sort of people write?" I asked.

"Well, about 70% are straightforward well-wishers, 25% cranks and 5% nasty cranks; most are autograph hunters. But all they'll get is my signature, and a cold message of thanks." My sympathies were with the autograph hunters; there was no harm in trying, I thought.

There remained one point on which we felt deeply and which Churchill had evidently found it inexpedient, if not discourteous, to raise. But at a Pilgrims dinner in front of several thousand guests and the press, Mr Kirk, the vice-chairman of Columbia University stressed it for him.

"It's illogical," he said, "for us Americans to expect other democratic nations to side with us, and at the same time to threaten to withdraw economic and military aid if the democracies show signs of not falling in 100% with American ideas."

"Hear! Hear!" Alan muttered. "He's nicely rounded off the political maelstrom of the past weeks." He sighed. "And now I can relax." Relax, I wondered, in New York?

24

The King was dead. In spite of knowing of his serious operation we were stunned, and it was some time after the phone call announcing it before, in silence, we began changing, Alan into a black suit and tie, and I entirely into black except for flesh-coloured stockings. We were now in court mourning.

"It's strange," I sighed. "He was such an unobtrusive, quiet man but I feel as though someone very close to me had died." Suddenly I was near to tears. "He remained with us in London all through the war. Under the bombs with his wife and girls. He didn't escape to Canada."

Alan put an arm round me, "I know. He was a decent man." Then he added, "We have to cancel all social and public engagements." I pulled myself together. So much had to be done.

First we scanned the papers for American reaction.

"Look at the headlines!" Alan exclaimed. "'The King is Dead'. Just as though it was their King," but I was shocked to read that the King, a very sick man, had slept alone. A King, but he had been left to die on his own. He may have groped for a hand or tried to speak. I did not like to think of it.

Newspapers, the radio, and people we met all expressed deep sorrow. It sounded genuine and it lightened my sadness. I felt that something precious was gone just when we needed it most. But I was amazed. I had expected indifference from Americans. It's incredible, I thought, with sickness and death taboo here, toughness and competitiveness admired, and the pursuit of happiness the American goal, yet the press is mourning the King for qualities Americans usually consider signs of weakness. The press was stressing what I had admired in the King. They wrote of his courage in remaining to face the bombs with his people, his devotion to his family and strong sense of duty. 'He was a good man', I read and it was meant as the highest praise.

The telephone rang continually as friends and strangers repeated, "We share in your country's grief," and "We admire the King." I was deeply touched and it kept me in a state of heightened emotion.

Newspapers devoted practically the whole of their enormous space to accounts of our Royal Family, of mourning in Britain and of the technicalities of the constitutional situation. Reporters besieged the office with questions such as 'How many Queens of England were there before Elizabeth II?' One lady expressed what many repeated, "It was so moving to see on television your new Queen returning from Kenya. She looked so young in that simple black dress, and to see that old warrior, Churchill, bowing low to his Queen! I wish she was ours!"

The King's funeral was watched by most people live on television and it was rebroadcast time and time again. New Yorkers crowded into the Episcopal Churches for Memorial Services. All over New York, churches tolled their bells fifty six times, the age of the King, a mournful, harrowing sound, and in Philadelphia, at noon, as the funeral service began in London, the famous Liberty Bell rang out. It had proclaimed America's freedom from Britain and now it rang out for a British King.

As Alan and I entered St Thomas's church on Fifth Avenue, we heard the final funereal tones of the bell that had tolled at one minute intervals. It was sombre inside and candles threw deep shadows across the arched columns. We were led through a packed church to a front pew. Behind us United Nations delegates and Commonwealth representatives sat silently. It was a solemn, dignified service. Alan's voice was loud and grave as he read the lesson from the Corinthians and spoke of 'corruption and incorruption', of 'mortality and immortality'. As the Rector, displaying the King's Medal for Service, paid tribute to the dead monarch, the atmosphere was heavy with emotion. Women wept, my throat contracted, and I had to keep back tears. At the end the whole congregation stood very straight as the church resounded with the singing together of our two National Anthems. Trinity Church, where Mr Hobson read the lesson, was so crowded that people had to stand in the aisles and in the gallery.

As we drove home, I yawned, emotionally exhausted.

Alan remarked, "I got through that all right."

"You said 'bodies terrestrial and glory of the celestrial'." He smiled.

"I bet Hobson would have made more mistakes. I wonder what he was given."

Next morning a Herald Tribune headline read 'Bells tolled for gentle, modest Monarch'. I could hardly believe it. It reported that two thousand people had attended the service in St Thomas's. Describing events in Trinity Church the New York Times referred to 'Sir Henry Hobson'. "He would dearly like to be that," Alan exclaimed. "It's here, in this country of the common man, that he needs a title."

A Commonwealth colleague rang Alan to compliment him on his reading of the lesson, and Mrs Hinkler, in the office, gazed up at him and said, "You have a very beautiful voice." In my letter to his parents I had to add, 'P (Pomposity): in danger'.

We attended the actors' Memorial Service in the Church of the Transfiguration, commonly called 'The Little Church Around the Corner', so named because a minister of a fashionable church once avoided conducting an actor's funeral by saying, "There's a little church around the corner."

I was fascinated by the actors and actresses round us, all with solemn, sorrowing expressions that were almost too perfect. Basil Rathbone read the lesson. He stood tall and straight, his fine Jewish head bowed in sorrow, voice lowered, yet every word distinct. As he finished declaiming the mournful words, he raised long, thin fingers as though to bless us — a clergyman lamenting his King.

Laurence Olivier gave the address. For a tense moment he gazed far over our heads. Then slowly in a solemn voice, "Our King is dead . . ." he paused. "A great King of a great people . . ." Suddenly he unfolded before us a history of Britain, ennobled in a glorious Shakespearean flow. From the days of Magna Carta he showed England championing justice, the rights of the individual, fair play, "A noble land . . ." We sat entranced. "And England gave the world the greatest gift — the art of compromise." Then he stopped, and sorrowfully he breathed, "But this is summed up so often by the cruel phrase — British hypocrisy!" He could almost have wept and we, the congregation, with him. Then head high, wide-spaced eyes fixed onto the glorious distant future of our dreams, he proclaimed, "Ours is the fairest of lands, with a golden future . . ."

Vivien Leigh, his wife, in a front pew sat very still, very upright, her lovely head, to one side, cradled in soft fur, eyes lifted to his, the perfect listener. He was now standing head bowed, in silence. He had finished. I heaved a deep sigh and returned to a grimmer reality, but with a lightened heart.

Alan whispered, "Wonderful performance; only an actor could get away with that." But he was sincere, I felt sure. He believed what he had said only he could not stop acting.

With so many memorial services attracting crowds Mr Hobson was worried. The Commonwealth Consulates Memorial Service in the Cathedral was fixed for February 20th. The King had died on February 6th. "It's too late. They'll have forgotten him. No one will come," he kept repeating.

"The invitations have gone out, Sir" Alan said firmly, "It's too late to change dates." They were in the Cathedral with Canon West, discussing seating and other arrangements.

"We'll be turning them away. There'll be no more standing room, you'll see," Canon West reassured Mr Hobson and winked at Alan. He looked severe with his bald head and pale face but he invariably relieved solemn occasions with a dry wit that Alan found refreshing. It was a tense time for Alan. Whatever the Commonwealth Consulates undertook, he had to do the work. As he said, "When there's work to be done, for 'Commonwealth C-Gs' read 'A.M. Williams'."

"The Duchess of Windsor is coming," Alan told the Canon. "We'd better double the number of police, and can you restrain the press from photographing her?"

"We'll tell them they can only take pictures of those taking part in the service." The press had raked up the whole tragic Windsor story. "But make sure everyone brings their ticket," and the Canon launched into one of his stories. "Mrs Manning, the late Bishop's wife, once forgot hers and when the police stopped her, she exclaimed, 'Young man, you must let me in. I'm Mrs

Manning, the wife of the Bishop'. The policeman stood firm, 'What a man! You're the fourth Mrs Manning today.'" Alan laughed but Mr Hobson continued to frown.

He turned to Alan, "You haven't forgotten the local authorities?" Alan shook his head.

"That reminds me," the Canon was irrepressible. "When a local politician, Mr Tuttle, made a speech and was acclaimed a really outstanding man, in his car on the way home he said musingly to his wife, 'I wonder how many really outstanding men there are in the world today?' To which Mrs Tuttle replied, 'One less than you think, dear.'" Mr Hobson smiled politely and the Canon winked again at Alan.

Well before eight o'clock on the evening of the 20th, we slipped in through a side door of the Cathedral. It looked enormous and I understood Mr Hobson's fears. Alan left me in a second row from the front and went off to lead in the VIPs: the Soviet UN Delegate, the Iranian, the Egyptian. People were streaming in and the Cathedral quickly filled up. Five thousand people were present according to next morning's papers.

At the last moment Alan led in the Duchess of Windsor, a slim figure in black, a black veil covering her head down to her shoulders. She was followed by her companion. They walked quickly into the pew in front of me, with British officials from the UN and the Consulate stepping in on either side to shield them. I stared at the Duchess's back. Her girlishly tight waist contrasted with the sagging lines round the corners of her jaw and the long, pointed chin.

The service started, solemn, dignified and I found it harrowing with the familiar mournful tunes reverberating through the Cathedral. The Australian Ambassador in mourning clothes rose to read the lesson, as Sir Oliver Franks was down with influenza. The Bishop of New York gave the address but I could not listen, for those slim, slightly stooping shoulders in front of me were heaving. The Duchess slipped a handkerchief under in her veil. Head bowed, she tried to control her sobs. The photographers had obediently turned their backs on the congregation and concentrated on the Bishop, the Canon and their acolytes. I felt sorry for her. I remembered what an American friend had said of the Duke. "If that fellow had done his job, the King would probably still be alive today." Most of us British would have agreed. The Duchess was probably the cause of the King's death. He had not been brought up, and was not suited, to be King. The strain had been too great. But now with the Duke attending the King's funeral in London, she was facing the sorrow and the criticism alone, and I was glad we were there to protect her. At the end Alan led her quickly out through a side door.

We had done our duty by our King. Cut off from home, strangers wherever we were sent, our country and our King meant a great deal to us. But New Yorkers had mourned the King with us. They had shown the same respect and admiration, and I had learnt that if there is much that divides us from America, there is also a great deal that unites us.

25

Now we had four months of mourning. We were instructed to entertain only small groups, and informally, which was tricky. Sometimes twelve or so guests sat gloomily around. Cocktail go-ers are out to display their finery, to be seen by, and to see VIPs but as guests drifted in at different times there was no crowd to admire them or on whom to make an impression; they wilted.

If the party went well however, guest flinging witticisms in a continual stream stayed on and on till I was forced to whip up a ham and salad supper and we were drained of sparkle by the time they left. We tried holding a general discussion but too many had to sit listening and that they found boring. If different subjects were discussed the one you were not engaged in invariably sounded more interesting. I overheard,

"What power does the Queen have?"

"She's the most permanent, most influential . . ." and it was difficult to concentrate on my, "We depend on international trade . . ." But we struggled on never knowing whether the next party would be a success or a flop.

Friends from Reykjavik, the Siggurdssons, dropped in for a drink. Alan had been posted in Iceland during the war. Sigurdur, a tall man with a square head, lowered his heavy bulk into an arm-chair, sipped his whisky and looked us over in silence through round-rimmed glasses, while Karistas, his wife, plump and matronly smiled beside him. Accustomed to Americans bursting into speech, I waited, puzzled. The only sound was Sigurdur topping up his glass. The whisky bottle was beside him. Mamoo came in and looked at us in astonishment. When the Sigurdssons left, she exclaimed, "You should encourage them to talk, choose subjects that interest them." Alan laughed. "We'll put you next to Sigurdur when they come to dinner." Mamoo nodded assent.

We invited Vania and Mr Bryan, the Canadian Deputy Consul-

General to meet the Sigurdssons. Before they arrived Alan remarked gloomily, "The Sigurdssons are apt to form pools of silence and neither Vania nor Mr Bryan are exactly fountains of small talk any more than I am, but we'll see how Mamoo fares."

We sat down, Sigurdur beside me, Mamoo on his other side. "I understand you are going on holiday to Bermuda?" she began. Sigurdur grunted. "Have you been there before?" He shook his head. "A lovely island." She had never been there either. The rest of the table talked quietly, conscious of Mamoo's efforts. She tried again, "You knew Alan in Iceland?" Sigurdur nodded. They were silent a moment. Then, "Do you know America well?" Sigurdur took a long swig at his wine, put the glass down, wiped his mouth, stared at his plate and answered, "No." Mamoo smiled at him, but wanly. She looked tired; Alan and I grinned. She went on trying, eliciting grunts and nods. Finally Vania came to the rescue, and he and Mr Bryan talked across the Sigurdssons. As soon as the meal was over, Mamoo pleaded tiredness — she had cooked the dinner — and fled.

The Sigurdssons invited us to dinner at the Waldorf. Sigurdur presented me with white carnations to pin on to my black dress. Seated at a corner table, a chandelier above and tiny pink shaded candles on the table, Sigurdur kept filling our glasses as we enjoyed course after course, chewing placidly. The only conversation was "Isn't this good?" and "Some more?" It was the first such silent meal I had ever had; it felt companionable, and relaxing. When a photographer aimed his camera at us, I automatically put on the social grin and Alan too, but Sigurdur and Karitas remained their natural selves. Looking at the photo later, I saw how unnatural I looked, and in a flash I understood why our trip to Washington had been so unrewarding. My colleagues, the diplomatic wives, were all putting on an unconscious and deeply-rooted social act. They were like marionettes and I found this boring and unhelpful. I remembered a Burmese lady telling me that she found it trying in London as she was expected to talk only about flowers or the weather. She had no garden and never noticed the weather.

As for public functions, we were told to attend them but to wear mourning and not to dance. Invitations crowded in but

Alan and myself with Sigurdur and Karitas Siggurdssoon in the Waldorf Astoria

since most were repetitions of the previous year they were less of a strain and I enjoyed them. There were always something unique about every occasion, something that was either significant, delightful or amusing.

For St David's Day dinner in the Waldorf Astoria we invited Kapa and Katia. Katia, in a long lace gown with large pearls rounds her slender neck and several heavy gold chains on her wrist, looked very distinguished even among the be-jewelled ladies in gorgeous dresses.

Over the hors d'ouevres, Kapa, with a self-satisfied grin, entertained our table with his latest theory, "We're told to help India. But would you believe it, there are twenty-five million monkeys there. I have the figures. And seven million 'unproductive' cows. They eat more food than the USA and Britain together could ship out there. And the Indians don't kill them because of their religion. I say, they've got to change their religion."

"And what about the wastefulness over here, you were on about," Alan retorted, springing to the defence of a Commonwealth country. "All those tons of precious tins that are thrown away daily?" The speeches began and Kapa did not have to answer. We continued eating our lobster salad in silence.

A revivalist Welsh preacher rose to his feet on the dais. He stood silent so long that guests stopped eating, looked up and met a stern gaze.

Suddenly he bellowed into the microphone, "There you sit, dressed in all your finery, in this luxurious hotel, filling your stomachs." He glared down at us, "What about your duties? Do you cast your vote? Take part in the government? Does Harlem distress you?" He seized the microphone and his voice quivered into it. "Do you share your wealth with the poor? With the Negroes?" We were now about to start on the steaks we had been served when he jabbed a lean finger down at us and shouted,

"You sit here eating enormous steaks while the poor of the world starve. Have you no conscience?" I put down my knife and fork, overwhelmed by guilt. In our last post in Iraq, I had been sickened by pitiful beggars and children who were all bones. Others hesitated and exchanged glances, uncertain whether to stop or to continue eating. I was suddenly conscious of Kapa, leaning back in his chair, eyes closed. He had a knack of snatching sleep at odd moments and waking refreshed.

"I say to you," the preacher shouted, "Give your steaks to the poor!" Kapa's mouth fell open, and he gave a gentle snore, loud in the ensuing silence. Katia and I exchanged glances. He was on the other side of the table so we could not wake him. We tried not to laugh, but the preacher's spell was broken. He was concluding, "May the Almighty give you courage to do what needs to be done." We bowed our fashionable hair-does over our plates. "May He lead you and give you strength to break with your selfish ways." He sat down. A sigh went up but no applause. It had been almost a blessing. The preacher frowned, disappointed.

Where was the rapturous clapping? Kapa woke with a start and exclaimed, "What's that?"

Next Lord Samuel addressed a meeting of the American Friends of the Hebrew University. We, Distinguished Guests, stood on the platform with him while the whole assembly sang with gusto the Israeli National Anthem. It was strange to find myself, embued as I was with all the traditional anti-semitic prejudices of a White Russian émigré colony, standing there, an honoured guest, surrounded by Jews. These prejudices had been shaken by the holocaust during the war, and now all remnants were swept away by the beautiful singing and the friendly faces round me. It seemed rude to stand facing this audience in silence so I mouthed the words and pretended to sing. Afterwards, the Israeli Consul at my side turned to me, "Congratulations! Fancy you knowing our National Anthem!"

Then we attended St George's Service in the Cathedral. Mamoo brought Libet to watch, as with banners unfurled, bag-pipes shrieking through New York's streets, and drums attracting all the little boys of the neighbourhood, the British 'Patriotic Societies' advanced on the Cathedral, Alan in morning dress marching in their midst.

At the Cathedral entrance Libet was prancing up and down with excitement. I entered through a side-door and not knowing where I should sit, went up to Canon West, standing at the entrance ready to greet the procession. I stepped up to him, just as the first banner-bearer came through the doors. Canon West swung his arms in a wide gesture of welcome and knocked me sideways. I was winded though I managed to keep on my feet. He turned and glared at me; I had spoiled his dramatic welcome. Coldly he pointed to the gallery above and meekly I betook myself there, keeping my face away from the congregation lest they should see me laughing.

That evening we were to attend the Shakespeare Society's Annual Dinner. Libet sent us off grinning as she ran up, singing out, "I know Shakespeare, 'Bubble, bubble, toilet trouble'!"

The following day, a South African reception I was to attend on my own. I was worried for Negro pickets had surrounded the hotel where it was to be held.

The Ulster-Irish 25th Annual Dinner. Alañis leaning back under the Union Jack and I am at the centre table with the off-the-shoulder dress, facing sideways

NNIVERSARY BANQUET
IETY OF NEW YORK, INC.
R   APRIL 25, 1952

DRUCKER-HILBERT CO.
N.Y.   2353

"Tell them you're Russian," my friend Mrs McCullough counselled. "They'll think you're a communist and they'll let you through." I did and it worked. Alan was not amused.

Then came the Ulster Irish Twenty-Fifth Annual Dinner. I sat below the dais with other wives of the VIPs above.

The Bishop of New York was the main speaker. His words sounded familiar; yes, it was the same speech he had made the week before at the Pilgrims' Dinner. He merely substituted 'Ulsterman' or 'Irishmen' for 'English-speaking peoples' and added a few Irish jokes. That's cheating, I thought, and he doesn't even look embarrassed. Alan, sitting beside him, was enjoying himself.

Suddenly I clutched the table. A mouse, plump and bristling with stiff whiskers, was crawling towards our table. Quickly I wrapped my long skirt round my legs and tucked them under me. I could not bear the thought of it running up me. My table-companions followed my gaze and immediately all lifted their legs and wrapped them up in the folds of their gowns. It was awkward bending down, without taking one's eyes off the Bishop. The mouse, frightened by the movement, darted under the table. We held our breath. My legs were stiff; I clung to the table edge. The mouse peeped out and walked slowly away. The Bishop glanced reprovingly at us. We lowered our legs and gave him our full attention. But only for a moment. The mouse was back. It darted in among us. Up went our legs. We clung to the table, shaking the glasses and spilling the wine. We did not dare move. The mouse came out, crawled away and disappeared. We relaxed. The Bishop had finished speaking.

And finally a Pakistani gathering. I found myself beside a group of women with dark eyes, black hair and dark skins that contrasted with their brilliant red, green and blue saris. I eyed them with curiosity — they were strange to me — and I listened.

"Mrs Roosevelt is here. She is being in the next room."

"Wonderful woman! What courage!"

"She is not caring who is criticising her. She is doing what she is thinking is right."

"And she is not looking down on anyone. She is respecting us just like her own folk."

"Yes, that's what people are not forgiving her for, that she is treating us as equals." I was taken aback and thought of my own supercilious attitude towards them.

There was sudden silence. A tall lady, dressed in a suit too tight for her ungainly body, with a big head, long face and a kindly smile, displaying large protruding teeth, had stepped quietly into the room. She began talking to a woman by the door. Eleanor Roosevelt. Among our American Republican friends she was labelled 'communist', the most insulting word in their vocabulary and was considered a traitor to her class. Suddenly I wanted her to know what the Pakistani women had said. As she moved towards another group, I stepped up to her,

"Mrs Roosevelt," I began and I introduced myself. "I just want you to know what these ladies have been saying," and I repeated their words, ending with, "You see, they admire and respect you and what you stand for." She looked startled, and uncertain how to receive the praise. We stood facing each other. Then as others came up, she gave a girlish giggle, squeezed my hand and said, "Thanky you, dear."

When I told Alan he was disconcerted and exclaimed,

"It's not done!"

"Well, it should be," I said. "Why are people praised only when they're dead?" and I took his arm and laughed.

Now at last a break. Katia invited us down to Bridgehampton for the weekend. "You can rest up and have some peace and quiet," she promised.

It was nearly spring. Azaleas had opened their velvety cups in the park and the highway to Bridgehampton would be a sensational sight, solid banks of pink and white dogwood.

26

We had to leave the children behind but they were busy playing a new game — Mothers and Fathers. We could hear Libet, "You give me money, my dearest," and Lawrence answered, "Yes, O.K. Fifty dollars, dear?"

It was cold in Bridgehampton and jumping out of the car I breathed in the fresh, salty, ocean air, such a relief after New York's overcrowded, overheated rooms. The old house peered at us, solid and welcoming from behind heavy, dark branches. The silence was restful. Here I need not think or feel anything. No more excitement or tension. I can let go and relax and, as Katia promised us — peace and quiet.

Katia and I changed into comfortable, bulky sweaters and thick skirts. We lit the drawing-room fire and piled logs on till it roared up the chimney. Then we hurried out into the garden to join our husbands. We found them hacking away at the apple trees. But should they prune when the sap is rising, I wondered, immediately anxious.

"Katia lets you cut anything you want; she seems to think whatever you do must be good for the trees," Kapa was grumbling. Alan's only reply was a self-satisfied smirk.

"I'm listening," Katia called out. "And I hate things being cut. They're more beautiful wild."

"Then why don't you direct operations?" Alan asked.

"No. Have your fun, and we'll see the results."

Hair flying, big eyes angry, Katiousha ran out. "You're chopping everything down again, the whole garden. Mama!" she protested. Katia drew her aside and whispered,

"It's good for them, darling. They need the exercise."

"But I want things as they are. I don't want them changed." Her mouth dropped as she watched one of the big branches crash down.

"It's my garden," Katia was firm, "so stop grumbling." Katiousha

172

thought a moment, then, "Well, if it does them good . . ." and she sauntered off, kicking at a stone with the toe of her plimsoll. I sympathsed and willed those apple trees to survive. Alan had strange ways of relaxing but there was nothing I could do about it. Better leave him alone.

I decided to help Katia tidy up the garden but I was distracted and entertained by Xana and her young men. She was attractive as ever even in old brown corduroy trousers and a Fair Isle sweater. Jean, a thin, narrow-faced Swiss, had bowed and clicked his heels when he shook hands all round. Now he escorted Xana on to the verandah. Jimmy, an Americn youth, tagged along behind them, pleading with Xana,

"Why not come for a ride in my car. Be a sport, Xana!" Jean ignored him and motioned a grinning Xana back inside. Jimmy followed closely. At the end of the day, a stony-faced Jean bowed to us, clicked his heels and left, while a victorious Jimmy sprawled over the drawing-room hearth rug.

Alan refused to come in till it was dark. Then he appeared his face grimy, twigs embedded in his curly hair and khaki sweater. "That was great!" he exclaimed as he ran upstairs to a hot bath. Then he laughed, "I only hope there'll be some apples this year." Katia's garden was crashing down, but Alan could do no more damage that night. I could forget the garden and settle down to a stimulating game of bridge after dinner.

We sat in front of the fire, Kapa, Katiousha, Alan and I. It was a traditional evening pastime, but as I might have foreseen the Nebolsines were in the midst of an argument. Kapa opened with 'One Heart'. Then he looked up at Katiousha.

"But how can you be sure the Gospels were written by Matthew, Mark, Luke and John?"

"It's a fact." Katiousha had a piercing voice. I had to raise mine for my 'Two Spades' call.

"They're eyewitness accounts. Three Diamonds."

"You can't know that. It's all surmise," Kapa shouted. She fixed him with big, earnest eyes and shouted back, "You don't go to church enough, Papa. You don't listen to the sermons."

Alan called loudly, "Three Spades," but Katiousha out-shouted him, "Our church never changes. It doesn't compromise with the present. It preserves the truth. We can trust and believe it."

"Papa, listen to Katiousha," Xana called across the room. "She knows what she's talking about."

If only they wouldn't shout. If only they would play properly, and I watched Alan drumming with his fingers on the table.

"Are you playing or talking?" Katia, who was bent over a jigsaw puzzle, demanded. "You're holding up the game."

"Four Diamonds," and Kapa got to his feet.

"Now where are you off to?" Katia asked.

"I'm hungry," and he stumped off.

"I'm hungry too," Katiousha cried and she followed him out.

"Four Spades," Alan called after them, adding under his breath, "Nebolisinery!" He dumped his cards on the table, leant back in his chair and glared at me — my relations! I looked away. Peace and quiet . . .?

Kapa returned munching a sandwich oozing ham and he carried a glass of whisky. He sat down. "Diamonds. Small slam." We all passed. With a wide sweep of his arms he spread out his hand.

"Papa you can't!" Katiousha cried. "You had no right to call at all. With only two small diamonds!"

"I say slam or nothing!" Kapa declared. I knew it would happen. Bridge always ended this way.

"You're impossible," Katiousha sprang up, flinging down her cards. "I'll never play with you again," and she rushed from the room, slamming the door behind her.

"Nebolsinery!" Alan repeated under his breath as Kapa took a long swig at his whisky and then suddenly grinned. I had to laugh too. Useless to expect peace with the Nebolsines, but it was a change from officialism, and there was never a moment of boredom!

Upstairs our room overlooked the front porch. As we undressed we heard whispering below. It was Jimmy's voice.

"All right, I'm going, but sure, you won't marry me?" The front door banged. Alan and I exchanged looks. Xana's young men!

But Katiousha worried me. "She's so narrow-minded," I told Alan.

"She'll grow out of it. She's and idealist; misplaced idealism, but it's good nevertheless." Yes, I thought, she loves her Russianness, the church and all it preaches. She defends everything connected with so-called 'Holy Russia'; she's loyal. But what high-mindedness!

Next morning, back in New York, Mamoo answered the phone. It was Katiousha, alone in their flat. "I feel so ill, Babushka," (Granny). Mamoo hurried over and found her slumped on a chair, very pale with dark patches under her eyes. She had eaten a whole plateful of cereal with cream, together with a pile of chocolate bars. Not always high-minded, I thought!

Next week-end Katia asked us specially to come down again. "Kapa's away and I need you, Alan," she said on the phone. Without Kapa, I thought, Bridgehampton might be restful.

Katia's self-control and reserve were proverbial but as we drove down, she kept twisting her wedding ring round and round her finger. Then at last she explained, "Xana's bringing a young man, Yuri Khlebnikoff. Don't say anything. I promised not to mention it — but he's asked her to marry him."

"How exciting!" I exclaimed.

"He's coming to ask my permission, as Kapa's away. That's why I need you, Alan." Then she laughed. "He's bought himself a new car, presumably to impress either me or Xana, I don't know whom."

As she had fallen silent, I pressed her, "Come on. Don't be cagey. Tell us about him. Has she accepted?"

She nodded. "They're Russian refugees like us. Yuri's doing very well as an interpreter at the UN."

We were all tensed up as Xana and her young man swept into the driveway in a large, shiny new car shortly after us. As they entered the drawing-room Xana gave a quick look round from under her dark brows and realised at once that we knew, but she said nothing. Yuri immediately made his presence felt. Unlike Jean and Jimmy he had poise. We could not help staring at him with his slightly protruding, very blue eyes in a handsome, haughty face and with a neat head of short fair wavy hair. His sturdy figure was clad in well-cut country clothes, not comfortable, delapidated ones like ours. He looks you straight in the eye, I thought. He's interesting, probably a handful, but I like him. To avoid an embarrassing silence we applied ourselves to our separate tasks in the garden. Xana and I began digging a flower bed.

Yuri hung around; then, "I'll split these for the fire," he announced, indicating a pile of logs. He set to, displaying considerable muscle as he swung his axe.

For something to say, I asked, "So that's a new car you've got, Yuri?" then I remembered that I should not have mentioned it. Yuri straightened up, stared reproachfully at Xana, who glared at her mother, who look reproachfully at me. Scarlet-faced, I dug deeply into the earth.

"Hi there, everyone!" Jimmy's little car ran along the driveway and out he bounced. But the sight of Yuri, the centre of attention, deflated him and he fell silent.

Over drinks and zakuski no one had anything to say. Katia went to the door and tried to indicate to Yuri a little summer-house at the bottom of the garden where they could have their discussion in private but he paid no attention. Jimmy sat sulking in a corner and I was afraid of saying the wrong thing again. As we waited the only sound was the clink of our glasses.

Yuri broke the supper-time silence by repeatedly asking in Russian,

"Is this fellow stopping here all night?" and he indicated Jimmy with a jerk of his chin and a disdainful expression.

As we washed up in the kitchen I noticed two red spots on Katia's cheeks. She had not been 'spoken to' yet and was angry.

"He's making himself too much at home. How dare he object to other guests?" He's bossy, I thought, but Xana will never be bored with him around. We got through a whole bottle of whisky that evening before going to bed, the family bidding a rather cool good-night to Jimmy as he drove off.

On Sunday it rained steadily all day. Alan woke up very stiff. We joined the others sitting self-consciously in the drawing-room. It was strange — no noise, no argument — this lively family sitting silently like statues, drinking. I found it more unnerving than their noisy arguments. Jimmy arrived at lunchtime but we were too tense to pay him much attention. After lunch, Katia turned to Yuri, got up and hurried through the teaming rain to the little house. Yuri hesitated, glanced awkwardly round for support, found us all looking the other way, and finally followed her. Xana ran out of the room. Jimmy got up too but Alan restrained him, "No, Jimmy, not now." We were left staring mesmerised through the windows and the rain at the little house.

At last Yuri emerged from it and we saw Xana run to him and as the rain pelted down on them, they sauntered, neat heads bent close together, round and round the lawn. Jimmy gave vent to a deep sigh, left the room and we heard his car drive off.

The young couple came in arm-in-arm, drenched to the skin. Xana's face was flushed and glistened under the rain drops; she looked very beautiful. They glanced round at our smiling faces but said nothing. Then they drove off back to New York.

"Well?" we turned to Katia. "Are they engaged? What did you say?"

"Yes. I agreed and gave my blessing," and irritatingly, face calm and reserved, she turned her attention back to her jig-saw puzzle.

In New York that night we found Xana sitting on our kitchen table, swinging her long legs and babbling away the happy news to Mamoo. "We're to be married in September. I'll put it in the papers tomorrow." Mamoo sighed and stroked Xana's head. Her first grandchild to be married. I kissed Xana; I too could not speak for emotion.

"I don't want Xana to get married," Libet exclaimed.

"I don't want her to go away." But next morning when Xana rang and asked for Libet, she shouted down the phone, imitating Mamoo.

"Yes. I'll carry your train and can I dress in white like you? With ribbon in my hair and white shoes and socks?"

Later I said to Alan, "She's only four. Will she manage? She's not used to Russian services and she'll be the only girl."

"Of course she'll manage. Stop fussing. The Russian church isn't all that different."

But isn't it? Alan was in for a shock. I had persuaded him to drive me down to Sea Cliff for a Memoraial Service on the anniversary of my father's death. He would enjoy the singing. The small church was hidden among trees, squat with a bright blue dome and golden cross above it. Vania had helped build it and Kaita had painted the 'ikonastas' or 'Golden Gates' that enclose the altar area. It was almost a family chapel and I wanted Alan to see it. We all assembled outside and then in we went.

I stopped short on the threshold and grabbed Alan's arm. In the middle of the church, an old gentleman in a dark suit was propped up in a coffin, his head resting on a cushion, silvery hair brushed neatly back, his cheeks over-pink, his waxen hands resting on a rug.

"His funeral takes place after our service," Vania whispered. Alan and I stayed at the back of the church. I wanted to protest. I don't know him, he's intruding. A corpse. I hate it and it's all made up, as if he wasn't dead. I could not resist peering at the body though at the same time I shrank from it. I could not concentrate on the service or enjoy my family's singing. I marked time till the service was over and we could hurry out.

"Barbarous custom!" I exclaimed outside. "A closed coffin is bad enough, but this is horrible." I felt cold in spite of the balmy evening.

"Churches don't change their customs overnight, Masha, my dear," Vania tried to pacify me.

A young American couple was standing smiling up at the church. "Let's go in and explore," the young man said.

"No, don't go in," I hastened towards them. "Just admire it from the outside."

"I'd like to see inside," the girl said.

"No, don't." Then I added, "There's an open coffin. A funeral is about to take place." Their smiles disappeared as they hurried away.

27

It was Easter but we were still in mourning as the temperature soared into the seventies, and cherry-trees and magnolia blossomed out along the park, a colourful setting for New York's Easter Parade. New York's ladies tripped down Fifth Avenue, displaying fantastic Easter bonnets. This year they outdid even Queen Mary with the bright vegetables and clusters of startling-coloured flowers balanced on their heads. On one lady's hat a live brown hen squatted clucking among green feathers, a single beady eye peering over its upturned brim.

It was my birthday and now I was free for the first time to spend it with the children. I praised their birthday card scrawls and arranged their three precious wilting leaves in a glass.

"Read to us, Mummy!" they begged. We settled ourselves on the grass on a shady verge in the park. The warm weather had brought out many families, making it safe. In a sing-song voice I read aloud from one of their books,

"This is the bread so fresh and sweet
That Betsy especially likes to eat."
Then, "This is the bread truck early each day
That comes to the market down the street
That sells . . ." The children beamed and joined in,
"The bread so fresh and sweet that Betsy . . ."

Other youngsters, uninhibited and curious, peered over my shoulder and soon a large group sprawled over the ground in their colourful play-suits, jostling us with chubby arms and legs, and chanting, "This is the loaf packaged so gay . . ." until we reached "the sticky, stretchy dough . . ." and finally we shouted out together, "the farmer on his tractor seat!"

The children clapped and shouted, "Again! Again!" and we started off once more while the parents sitting on benches nodded smiling.

At tea Mamoo lit five candles on my birthday cake — I was her fifth child. Libet, on her best behaviour, said, "Nanny, would you like to take your elbows off the table?" Mary giggled and removed her plump bare arms. Later the children acted for me. Libet rolled over the carpet, body stiff, arms at her sides.

"That's good, darling, but what are you?"

She frowned. "A rolling pin, of course. Now see if you can get this." She sat daintily picking, presumably fleas, off her arm, looking more like a cherub with her straight back, pink and white face and yellow curls.

"A monkey," I said as she jumped up to be hugged.

"Now me! Me!" Lawrence lay along the arm of the couch, arms and legs wound round it as he crawled forward.

"A caterpillar," I guessed. "That was very good." At that moment Alan walked in from the office and Lawrence sprang down and hurled himself into his arms, shouting, "My precious Daddy!"

Alan laughed as he caught him, "Gracious, what a long word!"

Our duties, owing to the continuing mourning, were not heavy. Alan had to present a flag to a church in New Jersey celebrating the two hundred and fiftieth anniversary of its founding. The normally monotonous, dusty roads had become pink and white bowers of cherry blossom, magnolia and dogwood.

We entered one of those little white wooden churches with slender steeples that dot the American countryside. The royal crown, surmounting the steeple was pitted with bullet holes from the time when the southern rebels tried to shoot it down.

The congregation was festive. The ladies in light-coloured spring suits and Easter bonnets made me feel dowdy in my black dress. After the appointed hymn, Alan, solemn-faced, advanced slowly up the aisle towards the altar, the folded flag in his arms. He unfurled it, bowed and offered it to the clergyman.

"Hold it! Again please!" A press photographer! Taken unawares, Alan laughed out loud, then quickly he pulled himself together and glanced at the priest who nodded, handing the flag back. Then to the clicking of the camera Alan presented it a second time.

Later he was annoyed with himself for laughing.

"But they don't mind," I consoled him, "They're not as formal as we are." But I chuckled all the way home.

We attended a spring ceremony in the American Academy of Arts and Letters, and gazed with others at the lions of the American literary world; Pearl Buck, patrician, with her prominent, pointed nose and mass of hair brushed well back off an open, friendly face, Thornton Wilder, unexpetedly solid, square-headed, with beetling black brows and hawk eyes staring out from behind steel-rimmed glasses, and Carl Sandburg, round-faced, with the ruddy complexion of a farmer but the deep-set eyes of a visonary. The composer Aaron Copland was the main speaker. He was tall, slightly stooping, with a long, hooked nose and deep grooves from nose to mouth — a striking, eccentric lot. Copland surprised and delighted us. Before that vast audience he loudly proclaimed, "The uniformity that is imposed on us is stifling creativity . . ." and as he went on to speak of the general compliance with mediocrity and conformity, the tightly-packed audience leant forward, staring eagerly up at him, aware and exhilerated by the danger he was courting. Alan and I exchanged glances. It was a courageous speech. McCarthy was hot in pursuit of individuals in the artistic and literary world. Newspapers reported daily that film stars were banned from work for the left-wing beliefs they had held years before. The two prize-winners, Thornton Wilder and Carl Sandburg, both supported Copland in their speeches and the applause was tumultuous. It was heartening, especially as intellectuals as such were generally despised, if not actually considered suspect. It was the 'common man' who was revered. "Good for Copland," I whispered.

During the tea that followed we stood alone, knowing no one, till we recognised a clergyman and hurried up to him.

"Ah, there's Thornton Wilder," he exclaimed. "A fine author. Let us introduce ourselves." Alan backed away but the clergyman stepped up to the writer, introduced himself and insisted on bringing us up too. As Thornton Wilder moved off, after a polite, "Delighted to meet you," the clergyman exclaimed, "I've shaken his hand!" We were taken aback by this naiveté, but when he added, "Shaking their hands shows appreciation," we felt rebuked.

"That was brave of them," Alan said as we drove home. "Let's hope there were no F.B.I. agents present; they were sticking their necks out." How degrading it must be, I thought, for intelligent men to have to face the Committee on Un-American Activities.

"Why have Americans become McCarthyites?" I pressed Alan.

"Disillusion after the war, I suppose. Things not being as they were. Their solution to every ill, their God almost, is free enterprise and that, they think, is threatened everywhere by communism, so they blame the Russians."

"But why hound their own people?"

"Fear. They feel they've got to protect themselves. A nuclear bomb on Russia would be useless. It would only destroy a tiny corner of that vast land, and anyway the Russians have it too now, so they're trying to eradicate communism inside the country. They see enemies everywhere, in government, on the stage. They're hysterical and hysteria is catching. It's caught the whole nation." He fell silent. "Look at that," and Alan pointed out of the window. "Well-dressed crowds, pouring out of well-stocked shops, all the bustle of prosperity. That's free enterprise. Their life is good and they're afraid of losing it." But I remembered the hungry arabs in Baghdad, so poor they even stole our empty baked beans tins. Free enterprise doesn't feed them, I thought. Perhaps it feeds on them . . .

We met another victim of McCarthyism when Patricia Dunlop, my New Zealand colleague, invited us to dinner. "If you don't object to meeting Jack Service," she added.

"Who's he?" I asked.

"A high official in the State Department, an expert on China, but now McCarthy is out for their blood. Jack's lost his job and in Washington no one dares employ him. So he's come to New York. He registered in a hotel but as soon as they saw his name, he was told there was no room. He's staying with us, baby-sitting actually," she laughed. "That's all we can offer him but we know an English business man who might employ him. Jack Service has a wife and school children to support. You'd better consult Alan before you accept."

Good thing Patricia is not American, I thought. She couldn't conform if she tried. Denis Dunlop, tall and lean like Patricia, a cheerful boyish grin on his face, met us at the door. He was officially Vice-Consul, but also acting, unpaid C-G and the New Zealand representative at the UN. Patricia darted out of the kitchen in an apron.

"I'm nearly ready," she cried. Their flat was dark, the furniture scruffy, but they were warm and outspoken, and we trusted them. I had almost forgotten what it was like to speak without thinking carefully first.

Jack Service shook us heartily by the hand, a tall, distinguished man with the formal, considerate manners of the diplomat.

Another New Zealand UN official was there with a Chinese wife, a tiny, talkative lady, with a round Asiatic face, who sat perched on the edge of an armchair. She told me, "I have two Chinese children by my first husband and my present husband has two New Zealand children by his first wife, so we're building a house in Connecticut for us and the four children."

"Why so far from the UN?" I asked. She stared silently at her slim hands folded in her lap. "It's lovely there, of course," I ventured.

"No. It's because we're safer there. It's a 'mixed race' colony. For the children, it's best. Everyone's in the same boat there." It sounded more like a ghetto but she was smiling.

Our children are so safe, so protected, I thought, though I remembered how when I once took them to the playground when we first arrived, they both fell unnaturally silent and kept close to me. Once inside, Lawrence, then only two, picked up a little girl's spade. She grabbed it from him and struck him hard on the chest. He fell backward into a sand-pit, picked himself up, stood a moment in silence, wiping sand off his face, then ran away, but not to me, and there were no tears. He had already learnt that it was each child for him or herself and each against the other. A hard lesson and I did not like it, but, I thought, I can't protect them from everything. They must learn to cope.

After a substantial meal of steak, roast potatoes, mushrooms and peas followed by my favourite chocolate mousse, Denis, flushed from the brandy, leaned forward, elbows on the table. "McCarthy's terrorising the American members of the UN," he said angrily. "They daren't put forward unpopular opinions. They're afraid of losing their jobs. It's monstrous. They've hounded one man in the Secretariat to his death. He threw himself out of a window. It's shaken us all."

Patricia shivered, as we fell silent.

"You daren't speak the truth," Jack Service said quietly. "I reported back home that Mao would probably defeat Chiang Kai-Shek and as a result lost my job."

"Mao cares more for the people," the Chinese lady interrupted. "Chiang only cares for political power." Yes, I thought, she'll be safer in her mixed-race colony.

"And now," Jack Service continued. "I'm blamed for the fact that Mao did win."

"How can they expect State Department officials to submit objective reports?" Denis almost shouted. "This'll gag them for years to come."

"It's tragic," Jack Service sighed heavily. "Even Dean Acheson, the Secretary of State, is suspect." He spoke dispassionately, with no appeal for sympathy. I admired his self-control, but under the surface, I thought, we're all vulnerable, especially when there are children, and I hoped fervently that he would get that job. I kept seeing the dead body sprawled under a UN window. Denis refilled Jack's glass and Patricia leant protectively towards him. And yet, I thought, America, Russia, they're both basically idealistic, their profesed aim is the same — the welfare of the world's people, yet here we are at each other's throats, disagreeing on how this should be achieved.

The last day of official mourning coincided with the children's end of term party at their Central Park school. Mamoo, Mary and I sat with the other mothers, each one beaming, enthralled by her own child. It was a balmy, sunny day. When, with the beating of drums and the clash of cymbals, the tiny tots marched on, I will always treasure the sight of my Lawrence heading the procession clasping the staff of the Star Spangled Banner to his bulging tummy in its light blue playsuit, his round, mischievous face screwed up into solemnity. And then amidst the pretty summer frocks and coloured ribbons, Libet skipping round the maypole, her plump face alight with joy and laughter, fair curls bouncing

Central Park School party

off her shoulders.

That evening as I dressed in black for the last time, I said to Alan, "It was lovely in the park watching the children, and the world seemed so normal."

28

"Our landlord is selling this flat and we have to get out," Alan announced.

"Oh no!" I cried. "That's too much. Not all that packing and unpacking again! Alan, I can't do it. Why don't they provide us with accommodation like the armed forces? At least we'd survive." And I shouted, "I know! I know! There's no precedent. Precedence, conventions, bureaucracy, annual accounting, I'm sick of the lot!"

"Never mind, calm down, Masha! We've got till September."

"Marvellous! So on top of everything else I have to hunt for a flat."

Mourning was over and the summer was upon us with June's social engagements and no time for anything else. New York was sweltering in temperatures of 92 degrees with humidity at 100%. At a Chamber of Commerce luncheon we suffocated in the overcrowded hotel dining-room, our formal clothes clung to us and it was hard to keep awake after the heavy roast beef and sauté potatoes.

At an Australian dinner our exhausted hosts gave up watching their language and everything became 'bloody this' and 'bloody that'. Even the Consul-General turned to me with "This bloody Churchill of yours", though I knew he admired our Prime Minister. At the Veterans' Commonwealth Ball, the shrill piping of the Yonkers Kiltie Band in the confined space reverberated through my hot, throbbing head and I had to sit down to recover. Alan, emerging from his dentist's air-conditioned surgery into the heat of the street, exclaimed, "The street's like an oven. That's the way to catch a really beastly cold." Air-conditioning will obviously have to come, I thought, a boon for many but it'll widen still more that gap between Park Avenue and Harlem.

We showered the children several times a day but still they

itched from a heat rash and had to be changed time and again during the night. Tempers became frayed and Mary nagged them. Once at breakfast she burst out, "Oh, do shut up and get on with your cereal!"

Lawrence exclaimed, "Oh my poor cross love!" Mary hugged him, "I'm sorry but it's this heat. I've lost all the patience I ever had."

Then to cap it all Alan came home with the news, "We're losing the Thomases. They're being transferred to London."

"What? Such a short spell and they're off again?" I burst out. I could hardly believe it. The whole staff constantly on the move.

"It may be best for them," Alan went on. "Dorrie's prostrated by the heat and they can't get away. Nowhere to go, with no generous sister on Long Island. As for the Office, more changes again . . ." He sighed, and more work for Alan. Not wanting to add to his load, I said no more.

We had to give a farewell party for the Thomases. I tried to cool the flat by keeping the kitchen door and tradesmen's entrance ajar and by drawing the curtains against the sun. But the hundred or so guests stopped any flow of air and I wondered at their coming into such a steaming hothouse. Dark, damp patches spread over our clothing as we mopped our faces and gulped down drink after drink, but Dorrie, though very pale, continued to smile as usual. After the guests had left Wilfred drew fingers with that characteristic gesture through his unruly hair, roared with laughter and said,

"Thank you for a quite atrocious party!" That was the last we saw of the Thomases.

In the Birthday Honours List Hobson was made a KBE. He was away so we hurried round to congratulate the new Lady Hobson. She was radiant.

"He didn't tell me, the old oyster!" she cried. But Hobson had known nothing himself; the letter informing him of the Honour had been wrongly addressed so he was not given the customary chance to refuse.

"This heat won't worry 'Sir Henry', though it certainly would have laid plain 'Henry' low," Lady Hobson laughed. Hobson, I thought, has dignity and the Knighthood will suit him.

On July 1st, we at last escaped from New York, as Katia had again invited us to Bridgehampton. 'Everyone leaves New York in summer,' we were told. I pitied those millons not included in that 'everyone'.

We scrambled out of the car in Bridgehampton into a cool, fresh breeze, and soon we were floating in the ocean, its waters transparently clear with little silvery ripples breaking over us, and with nothing in sight except sands shimmering in the heat, and pale, green dunes stirring gently in the wind.

We settled into our usual routine of bathing, bridge, eating and sleeping, Mamoo and I taking turns again to stay with the children and when it was my turn to remain in New York, I hunted feverishly for a flat.

I hated those journeys back and forth in the Nebolsine car with Alan driving. He kept trying to beat his two and half hour record but, by night, lights from the stream of oncoming cars dazzled him, and by day, he tried in vain to rush past the numerous vegetable stalls at each of which Kapa hoped to buy sweet corn, his favourite vegetable, just a wee bit cheaper.

"Stop! Stop here!" Kapa shouted as Alan sped on, and I clung to my seat, pressing hard down on my left foot, cursing this mania for speed. Life was tiring enough without this added strain.

The house filled up with a Russian crowd and Mamoo suffered with us as they voiced pro-German sentiments. Forgetting the 1939 German-Soviet pact, they maintained, "The Germans were right; they opposed the Soviets all along." A Russian Prince, now a university lecturer, accused all his colleagues of being 'reds' and he told Mamoo, "Churchill is dangerous man; was he not a Bolshivist in his youth?" Mamoo also overheard his saying, "The common man is no concern of mine." Work, in general, he despised, but "One has to eat!"

Alan commented, "Small wonder there was a revolution in Russia," but Mamoo protested, "These Russians here are the last ditchers of the worst type." But perhaps, I thought sadly, the snobbishness gives them the illusion of still being 'somebody' and so keeps up their morale. Mamoo escaped into the kitchen and calmed herself by cleaning vegetables.

Alan muttered, "Bigotted snobs," and he too escaped, but into the garden.

Alan had his summer mapped out, "I'm going to build a Welsh dry wall," he informed Kapa. In shorts, their bare backs soon smeared with mud, they heaved at large stones.

"But why not use cement?" Kapa specialised in laying cement.

"It's a dry wall; the stones must fit together." Alan's nose was already peeling and the backs of his ears and neck were a bright red. I had had more sun and was well browned over. Alan was content as he muttered, "These damn stones . . ."

The children made a scarecrow to protect the grass seed he had planted. Mamoo came past and without looking up she addressed it, "Alan, I think you should . . ." The children bounced up and down with glee.

One elderly professor stood out among the Russians there. He peered out from behind the thickest glasses and his upper lip was permanently raised in a good-natured greeting to all and sundry. Hurrying across the lawn to greet us, his feet dislodged one after another the croquet hoops which had just been carefully measured out. That evening he turned on what he thought was the light switch on the standard lamp, only it was the canary's cage, and down it crashed with 'Sweetie' fluttering wildly inside.

"Dear me! What have I done?" was his constant refrain. Next morning he swam out to sea with strong, steady strokes, but he mistook the horizon for the beach and set off to reach it. Arkadi had to swim after him to turn him around. Luckily he was at hand. But despite his misadventures, the professor remained unperturbed and eager at any moment to discuss philosophy or religion — a true Russian and a favourite with Alan.

The main summer event was Xana's wedding. The day before, Alan brought Kapa up to Bridgehampton to give Katia a chance to cope with last minute arrangements.

From the house we could hear the roar of the ocean. We all ran down to the beach. Mountainous waves pounded it, biting into sand, sucking it greedily back. Four rollers, each growing larger than the last, surged towards us like an elaborate, gigantic fountain. We watched in silence, overawed.

A grey-haired man and a youth appeared in bathing trunks.

"Surely they're not going into that, Alan?" and I clutched his arm. As they ran past, they waved to us and the man smiled, bright blue eyes crinkling up against the brilliant sunshine. The boy grinned, mouth open with excitement. They waited at the water's edge, both lean and muscular, their bodies tanned a dark brown. They were studying the ocean, timing their entry. Then they were in, diving into one roller, then the second, third, fourth, and they were far away, splashing in the spray, beyond the breakers. Impressed, but uneasy at the danger they were courting, we went home.

We were eating lunch when suddenly a heavy vehicle rumbled past and on towards the beach. We rushed after it in time to see the 'duck', an amphibious lorry, hurl itself into thse huge waves. It was beaten back on to the sand, waves crashing over it.

"What's happened?" Alan asked a farmer, who had joined us.

"A man's in trouble out there." The duck tried to enter the water further down the beach, but the breakers forced it back again. Two aircraft were now skimming low over the water.

The farmer went on, "The man out there told the boy with him to get help. Guess he had a heart attack. The boy didn't want to leave him, but the man insisted. Must have known there was no hope. Probably saved the boy's life."

All afternoon the duck drove up and down the beach, struggling to break through the rollers while the aircraft flew back and forth above us. We watched helpless. That man struggling out there alone, grey head disappearing in the waves, arms and legs thrashing about, his body hurled around by stones, sand and water . . . I willed the duck to crash through the waves, the aircraft to spot him. I willed him to be saved. Darkness fell and the search was called off. He must be dead by now. Slowly we went home, and up to bed.

Kapa cried out, "What a thing to happen and just before Xana's wedding too!"

"Don't you know, Kapa," I assured him, "misfortune before a birth or a wedding brings good luck." An American woman had once comforted me thus. Unexpectedly, it had the desired effect and soon Kapa was snoring in his bed.

But I was wide awake. I no longer saw a blue-eyed man, but a repulsive corpse tossed about in the ocean. I shuddered and

Xana and Yuri with their groomsmen and Libet

wrapped the blankets closer round me. Nature can be so threatening, so terrifying, or are we too sensitive, I wondered. Perhaps we shouldn't think, just live like animals for the moment without imagining pain and fear. Americans fill every moment of their lives. Is it to escape thought? I wished Alan did not sleep so soundly.

Next morning Alan drove us all away from the ocean and back to New York, and in our flat the bustle of the wedding drove all sad thoughts away.

We found Katia standing cornered by two florists, both shouting at her, "You hired me for the job!" She fled to the kitchen leaving them to fight it out.

"Nebolsinery!" Alan grinned. We drove to the Russian Orthodox Cathedral. I held Libet's hand tight. She was smiling, sitting very straight in her white organdie dress with its full skirt below a satin ribbon belt and in white pumps and socks with a coronet of tiny white roses on her yellow curls. Perhaps I was more nervous than she was. Guests were crowding in. It was a fashionable wedding with a biship officiating. Xana arrived, her slim figure swathed in a billowing mass of ivory satin and lace, and a little lace cap with a flowing veil on her dark head. A bouquet of white roses and lillies cascaded down her dress. She smiled, her whole face lit up and I caught my breath.

As Xana swept into the cathedral, Libet carrying her train, her face serious, candelabra and candles sparkled on the silver and gold halos of the ikons. The choir burst into those lovely melodies that move Russians so deeply. Xana joined Yuri at the front of the church, a handsome D'Arcy-like bridegroom in his morning dress. We took up positions with the family. There are no pews in Russian churches.

Eighteen young men, a record number, I thought, formed up in two lines behind Xana and Yuri, and took turns at holding the heavy golden crowns over their heads, but my eyes were rivetted on Libet, so tiny as she bend down gravely and spread out the long, heavy train. Then she followd Xana three times round a small altar walking under the arms of the groomsmen and holding the corners of the train in her pudgy little hands. Then up to the rood-screen, still clinging to the train. She had not practised beforehand; she had only been told to 'hold the train'. I marvelled and admired!

Meanwhile Lawrence, in a white sailor suit, kept taking out his bosun's whistle. A stern look from Alan made him replace it. He then started fidgeting, standing first on one leg then on the other. "Mummy," he whispered, "I want to go to the . . ." Vania took his hand and led him away. When they returned Vania left Lawrence at the back of the church on a chair beside an old general. Throughout the service we could hear a high-pitched wail and a low rumble as they chanted with the bishop and the deacon, but no one minded.

After the service we hurried back to receive the two hundred guests. In the flat there was laughter, and shouting of 'gorko' meaning 'bitter' — a demand for the bride and groom to sweeten the drink with a kiss. Guests downed a hundred and eight bottles of champage (Kapa counted them).

"Will the floor hold, Masha?" A worried man came up to me. I

Myself, Katia and Natasha at Xana and Yuri's wedding reception

rushed in a panic to Alan who merely shrugged, "Nothing I can do now."

So Xana was married, the first of my nieces and nephews. She was not my child yet there was a lump in my throat and tears were welling up. I escaped embarrassed to the bathroom.

*   *   *

We still had one last week of the summer in Bridgehampton, and Alan was able to spend it with us. The four of us had the house to ourselves for we depatched Mamoo and Mary off on a holiday. We admired the dry wall that was now complete. Later it stood the test of a hurricane which brought down several of Katia's trees, and it still stands there today.

Rain pelted down forcing us indoors till, glancing out of the window, I saw a lake where the lawn had been.

"Run out children," I cried. "You can paddle on the lawn! Come on! Rain won't hurt you." They splashed in the water, rain pouring off them, and squealing with excitement.

"Look over there!" Alan called. A large turtle squatted at the edge of the water, its scraggy neck stretched out, its flat face turned up to the skies as it gulped down rain drops. It did not move as the children ran up laughing, squatted beside it, turned their faces up to the sky, and gulped down rain drops too. Then we watched fascinated as the turtle slowly raised its shell tö let in the wet.

When the clouds rolled away and the turtle wandered off we were back on the beach. Libet was carrying a rope.

Alan, "Where did you get that?" She hung her head.

Lawrence, "In a tent on the dunes."

Alan, "That was naughty. You must not take other people's things."

Lawrence, "I didn't know 'at I must not take other people's things.

Alan, "Well, you know now."

Lawrence, "Yes, I know now." Alan was stumped and Libet raised her head; it was she who had taken the rope.

On the last day we heard a loud throbbing in the sky. A flight of swans was moving fast and smoothly across it, with slow, steady wing-beats. Alan and the children stood gazing up, brown-skinned, relaxed, smiling.

"We have to go with them," Alan said. "The summer's over."

29

We were installed in a new, comfortable, thought less elegant flat that I had found on Park Avenue. After the hullabaloo of moving and unpacking, Alan and I collapsed into deep armchairs to watch the American election results.

"Stevenson's the better politician," Alan remarked. "The better intellect and probably the better administrator, but people invariably think they can vote themselves out of trouble and that's what he's up against; and then the Democrats have been in too long. And, of course, Eisenhower, the national hero is far, far better know."

On the T.V. screen we studied Stevenson's long, scholarly face and eyes which seemed to search the horizon far above the 'common man' — America's ideal. In contrast Eisenhower looked more down to earth with his square head, stocky figure and homely smile. Eisenhower won the election.

Alan sighed, "It's disappointing but not disatrous. Eisenhower's a good man."

For me the campaign had been momentous. Whenever I was home I turned on the radio, and first I heard all the political salesmanship, with familiar appeals to greed and a cynical play on prejudice and fear. "Senator Smith is a thief and defender of communists," and General Marshall was labelled 'a living lie, a front man for traitors.'

Then suddenly a new voice. "Let's talk sense to the American people. Let's tell them the truth that there are no gains without pain. Better we lose the election than mislead the people." Adlai Stevenson, Governor of Illinois! How exciting and refreshing! An echo of our friend Mrs McCullough, and as Democratic Presidential candidate he must be speaking on behalf of millions of Americans. I carried the radio round with me. Stevenson condemned the "insensate worship of matter," and called on the country to "triumph over the great enemies of man — war, poverty and tyranny." He explained his reason for entering politics, "Why is it," he asked, "that 'Fight, suffer, die, squander our substance — yes; but work in peacetime for the things we die for in war, no!?'" I heard again my brother Vania saying, "Politics are dirty and dishonest."

But Stevenson's America is not like that, I thought. He might even be able to deal with what he called "the grim problems of war and peace which weigh so heavily on all of us today." He dared to attack the McCarthyites, "Too often sinister threats to the Bill of Rights, to freedom of the mind, are concealed under the patriotic cloak of anti-communism." As I drove throught the city, I glimpsed Americans glued to their radios as they munched sandwiches in drug-stores or leant against bars, manhattans in hand. Their radios blared out of cabs and even silenced gossip in the barbers' shops.

"Hear! Hear!" I murmured repeatedly, as Stevenson maintained, "Our country was built on unorthodox opinions. My definition of a free society is a society where it is safe to be unpopular."

I wondered what Americans made of his Churchillian eloquence. "Where we have erred, let there be no denial, where we have wronged the public, let there be no excuses. Self-criticism is the secret weapon of democracy and candour and confession are good for the political soul."

Though he lost the election his words were not wasted. They had resounded throughout the United States and all at once I gained an insight into these multi-cultural, thoroughly mixed-up people of the United States, molded into superficial conformity yet all straining in different directions. We can be friends, I thought, and allies, but they are virile, stronger than us; we must be careful never to become subservient — that's the danger.

I tried to convey these conclusions to Mrs Godwin, the new Consul's wife, when she called and sat on the edge of her chair, a neat, anxious woman in a new posting. "New York is the world in miniature," I said. "It's got all its riches and problems, virtues and vices. They're all here, displayed before you." I wanted to spare her the confusion and insecurity I had felt. She was gazing up at me nervously and I reassured her, "You'll find it fascinating," but I also had to warn her, "It's hard living, very hard. Not a moment to yourself and you have to fight to survive!"

With this new understanding I no longer felt a stranger in New York. With two years' experience I felt I could deal with whatever problems arose and with whatever was expected of me. For the first time I felt I could give of my best. I was no longer tensed up. I could relax, enjoy New York, and keep fit.

I tackled the job in a new spirit. The bazaar, with Mrs Godwin's help, became an amusing and friendly affair. Libet was to present to Lady Hobson the 'nest-egg' (the money collected by the Victoria Home at their annual garden-party). I held her hand reassuringly during 'God Save the Queen' as we stood in the front row of the hall, and I squeezed it tightly and gave her an encouraging push when the loud-speaker announced 'Elizabeth Wiliams'. She looked enchanting in a short white dress with a full skirt and a big white bow on her hair. She climbed up the steps on to the stage, clasping the large egg, and curtsied as she presented it to Lady Hobson. Then to loud applause she turned to come down again. She lowered one little foot but the step was too high. She tried the other foot but it was too difficult. There she hovered, eyes wide with distress. Instinctively I half rose, but a murmur ran through the hall, an official hurried forward, took Libet's hand and she was able to step down. As the audience smiled and applauded, I gave her a hug.

I even felt confident enough to help the Hobsons, something I had been unable to do for the Evanses. At the film premiere of 'Breaking the Sound Barrier', as Lady Hobson was absent, I sat next to Sir Henry in the front row with the VIPs, instead of with Alan further back. Sir Henry was still new to the job and felt more at ease with one of us beside him.

Before the film started he was introduced to the public, but as 'Sir Harry Hopkins'. His bushy eyebrows shot up but, wiping sweaty hands on his handkerchief, he strode up on the stage. After the briefest of speeches down he rushed again like a homing pigeon. He was followed by the hero of the film, the pilot Yeager, who was introduced as 'This bravest of men — first to fly faster than sound, who will now say a few words.' We watched Yeager, a slight figure, as he stood before us on the stage, face pale, eyes darting hither and thither over the audience, and his lips trembling as he stammered, "Er . . . I . . . er", and unable to say another word, he fled off the stage. Sir Henry sighed heavily with relief, mopped his brow and we both laughed.

There was a slight embarrassment between Sir Henry and myself. At a party to celebrate his Knighthood, I had stepped down off a flight of stairs straight into his arms which he was holding out in greeting, and without thinking we kissed. Lady Hobson and Alan stared at us with raised eyebrows. Quickly I disengaged myself from his arms and muttered to Alan, "It was just a kiss . . ." He remained oddly silent and I escaped into the crowd of guests.

None of us was ever quite sure of the charming but irascible Sir Henry. Once when Wilfred Thomas was standing in for him at a ceremony in a theatre, the loud-speaker announced 'Sir Henry Hobson' and the spotlight picked out the box in which Wilfred sat. He dropped to his knees and grovelled on the floor leaving an empty box for the audience to admire.

"I wasn't going to risk being accused of impersonating the C-G," he later explained.

I now looked forward eagerly to the large, official receptions and no longer felt overwhelmed by them. At a cocktail party given by Sir Gladwyn Jebb in honour of the United Nations delegations gathered for the General Assembly, I left Alan of my own accord and 'did my stuff' as he put it, on my own. I found myself in the wrong queue and shaking hands a second time with Mr Eden, the Foreign Secretary, the guest of honour.

"Sorry! It's me again," I told him unabashed. "Got into the wrong line." I was amused to notice him clinging on to Alan's sleeve to hold him till another group of guest approached. VIPs evidently also felt nervous and foolish when left to stand by themselves.

When he was released, Alan laughed, "At least I've served a useful purpose but I don't suppose it will get me promotion!"

I gaped with interest at the VIPs, at Mrs Roosevelt's large, angular figure with a heavy face, head inclined in friendliness towards her companion, Krishna Menon, with his great mop of wiry hair and brilliant eyes in a lean, brown face. Vyshinsky, the Soviet delegate, a pale, elderly little man could only be glimpsed between three toughs with bulging pockets, one on either side and the other behind him. Colleagues could only approach him from the front. No one else, I noticed, even tried. He stood there ostracised and I felt ashamed for him. No other delegate brought armed bodyguards to a private party. There was surely no danger in Sir Gladwyn's home where we were responsible for security. If they dared not take the risk, then surely his guards could be camouflaged as guests. This Soviet paranoia about security . . .

In between these autumn receptions, which I was now able to take in my stride, I decided to give the children a combined birthday party. "They never see us, Alan," I told him. "I must do something for them, and I've been longing for a children's party."

Mamoo and I prepared mounds of sickly, creamy pastries. We had two cakes, one with four blue candles and the other with five pink ones. The sixteen children cleared the cake plates in no time and then, in spite of their sophisticated life-styles, I was surprised and pleased to find them enraptured with the little presents of coloured pencils and tiny balls. We played games and they sprang up and down to musical bumps while Mamoo played the piano. Later I started a different game and told them to pretend to be dogs. Mamoo misunderstood and thumped out a loud tune just as all the children fell on to all fours and began barking for all they were worth. The noise was shattering. I was sure the neighbours would complain and we would be thrown out. I tried to shake Mamoo's shoulder as I waved frantically to the children to be quiet. But it was some time before the uproar subsided. The children collapsed laughing on the floor and one youngster exclaimed, "Boy, was that good!"

Just before Christmas the English Speaking Union gave a recepiton for Mr and Mrs Eden. I looked forward to seeing the Mrs Eden. About a thousand guests formed up into three queues to be introduced. The ladies, excited, dolled up in their smartest suits and hats, jostled each other as they pressed forward. Suddenly all three queues lurched simultaneously towards the honoured guests. The ladies in front were flung up against the Edens, almost knocking them off their feet. Mr Eden was recovering from an operation. Alan hurried to his aid and led him quickly away. I immediately pushed my way through to Mrs Eden, and stationed myself firmly in front of her, protecting her with my shoulder against the advancing queues. I allowed the ladies through two at a time. Mrs Eden remained outwardly calm and poised as she shook hundreds of outstretched hands.

We were wedged up against a wall, almost surrounded, and with even less air than usual at crowded parties, but it no longer affected me. I was pleased with myself, cock-a-hoop. I had acted promptly and with assurance.

Next morning Alan was on the phone form the office, but I spoke first, "Alan, I really enjoyed myself last night and I managed all right when you left. I can cope now; it's such a relief!"

"Listen!" he interrupted. "We're off. To Tunis. I've just received a telegram. We're being transferred. I had to phone you but I must ring off now."

I clutched the receiver, speechless, my mind a blank. Then . . . Tunis! Where's Tunis? We're leaving? But we've only just moved into this flat. It's impossible and just when I can cope . . .

30

Tunis! I rush for the encyclopedia. 'Capital of Tunisia . . . Stands on a bay surrounded by lakes and marshes . . .' I push it aside. We're flung from post to post . . . the packing, the farewells, on top of everything else! My hands are shaking. Panic! I must control myself. I sit down and inhale deeply on a cigarette.

First things first. Accommodation in the UK.

"I must be in or near London," Alan says, "to wind up New York affairs and be briefed on Tunis, and we'll take our leave too. Then there's your shopping to be done."

Hotels are a misery with children and too expensive anyway. Perhaps a flat? Or better still a farm somewhere near London? Hurriedly we despatch letters to everyone we know who might help us to find something quickly.

"We're leaving, children, and going to a place called Tunis," I tell them. Libet goes red in the face and stands speechless. I sit her on my knee.

"It'll be all right, darling. You'll see. We're all going together." The children's routine will be broken, difficult food, climate, surroundings. Lawrence hates change, becomes fretful, whines, won't eat.

I invited their park friends to a farewell tea. Round-faced Ann wails, "I won't let them go. I'll lock 'em up so's they can't leave." And dainty Kate clings to my skirt, "I'm marrying Lawrence. Don't leave me behind. Please! You mustn't!" I stroke their heads.

"We're sailing on the Queen Mary," Alan tells us at lunch, and Libet remarks.

"Ships sometimes sink in the ocean."

"Don't! I hate ships and now I can't eat any more!" and Mary flings down her knife and fork and runs to her room in tears.

"I'll be C-G in Tunis!" Alan is excited. "We'll need our own car, a pompous one, perhaps a Humber Super Snipe." You and your cars, I think. You've been longing for one of your own.

Alan decided that three farewell cocktail parties will cover everyone with about a hundred guests for each, but we must give them before the packers move in. We write out invitations.

"We'll have to have all those injections again and even more for the children." I sigh. I tear open letters hoping for the Tunis Post Report. Until it comes we know nothing.

At dinner parties I grin and answer automatically, my thoughts elsewhere. What kind of clothes will we need? How hot is it in summer? But aloud I answer, "What can we British put into our common partnership? Well, for one thing there's our strategic position as an island off the coast of Europe. Then we have an army of some 850,000 men." Should I take long evening dresses? My black velvet? I mustn't buy the wrong clothes as I did for New York and waste so much money.

In bed I turn from side to side. So many problems; whether to bring furniture, what to send to Tunis and what for storage in London. Children will outgrow clothes if we're in Tunis long. I toss about restlessly. How can I plan, do anything when I know nothing? Steady on! I sit up, light the bedside lamp, get a cigarette and inhale.

Kapa and Katia's silver wedding party is crowded and noisy. I gaze sadly at my sister's face, with those lovely classical features, as she stretches out a jewelled hand to be kissed, and Kapa shouting, gesticulating, bottle in hand. No more 'Nebolsinery'! No more family. Alan and I will be again on our own. Mamoo is to stay in England and Mary goes back to Ireland.

"I wouldn't go to Africa, not for anything," she had said with a shudder.

Still no Post Report. I examine our clothes in the cupboards, collect what we need for the boat and London. It turns bitterly cold. 'Flu rages. We must keep fit. I chain smoke. Alan pours us out generous portions of whisky.

He receives a letter from his predecessor in Tunis. "Listen to this! 'The residence is a Beylical Palace,'" A palace! He goes on, "'Near La Marsa.'" An atlas, quick! Here it is, La Marsa, ten miles north-east of Tunis, beyond Carthage, and how tiny Tunisia is compared to the States! He reads on, "'Extensive ground . . . an irrigation tank which makes quite a usefull swimming pool,'" and then "'An electric tramway goes through the property with a stop rather grandly called "Consulat Anglais".' Sounds fantastic!" I'm beginning to look forward to Tunis.

I'm down with 'flu. Shivering, sore throat, sweating. Propped up in bed I draw up lists of what's to be done. The family keep putting their heads round the door.

Alan, "Are you better now, dear?"

Mamoo, "Are you getting up yet, darling?"

The children, "Feeling better, Mummy?" Still feverish, face red and swollen with catarrh, I crawl out of bed. I make piles of toys, knick-knacks, for packers.

"The Lord be praised, you're up and well," Alan exclaims. He is pale too.

The Princess Royal is hurrying through New York. Queen Mary is ill. Alan arranges a meeting with the Duke of Windsor in the Waldorf Astoria. I'm not involved so I can continue sorting, a large apron covering me from chin to knees.

Post Report finally arrives but with not a mention of clothes, furnishings, or climate. How can I decide what to take where? And time's running out.

"Alan, what shall I do?" I cry.

"Send everything to Tunis and to hell with it," Alan bursts out.

Our first farewell party. I put on the black dress with tiny white flowers embroidered over the skirt. Must keep up appearances. I smile and try to appear relaxed. Guests inevitably ask, "I suppose you will be glad (or sorry) to leave New York?" We grin and repeat, "On no!!" or "Oh, rather!" Iraqi C-G comes. We're very touched. It's four years since we left Baghdad, but I still feel it's part of me.

At the Edens' farewell party for us, an American woman journalist inveighs against McCarthy to Alan in a loud provocative voice. "He's a disgrace to our country . . ." Other guests shy away, leaver them standing alone. Alan nods appreciatively. He does not care now who sees or hears him.

Our second farewell party. Queen Mary's very ill. We're both in black just in case. I feel dramatic, part of history. Phone rings. Office ticker reports Queen Mary is dead. British and Commonwealth guests arrive with black ties. Alan slips out to put on his. A month of court mourning. Our third party is cancelled. What a break!

Day of funeral. After Memorial Service we're free and can get on with packing. In baggy grey flannels and his old tweed jacket with leather patches on the elbows, Alan lugs up trunks and cases from the basement on a trolley and into the dining-room, ready for the packers. I bring my sorted-out piles. Instead of carrying all our books Alan decides, "Easiest to move the whole case." Carefully he lowers it on to the trolley and leans on the handlebars with a self-satisfied smirk. He starts off from the study. The case shifts sideways. Books slide to the left. In the corridor they start slipping off. Bang! Bang! Faster and faster. The heavy Oxford Dictionary, Vol.1 crashes on to Peter Rabbit's face. Alan races for dining-room but books cascade right and left. He arrives with an almost empty bookcase. Alan's face comical in his dismay. I sigh. The rest of the afternoon spent crawling around the floor picking up books.

"My back's killing me," I complain. "What a silly thing to do! Balancing the book-case on the trolley like that!" I get to my feet.

"You never do anything silly do you?" and Alan gets up too. "It's always others who are to blame. My fault this, my fault that. I'm sick and tired of it! How should I know what they wear in Tunis or what the climate's like? I don't care a damn anyway!" He's shouting. We face each other. He glares at me, hating me.

"No, don't. I can't stand it!" I'm in tears. His arms are round me. He's laughing. "Sorry!" He kisses me. "Remember. Foreign Service maxim — last three weeks at a post anything's permissible short of actually scratching, slapping or pulling hair." I smile.

"O.K. I know. I forgot." I flop on to couch, and reach for the inevitable cigarette. Alan hands me a whisky.

"Now I've got to dress for dinner, and I'm worn out," I exclaim.

"We'll help," the childen cry. Libet runs my bath, hands me my clothes. Lawrence answeres the phone, "Mummy's worn out. Sorry. Bye!" They fasten my gold sandals and spray me with perfume, and before I put on my fur coat, Libet runs to lower the toilet seat for me.

Leaving New York on the RMS Queen Mary
Myself, Libet, Lawrence, Mary and Alan

Measles at park school. Our children in quarantine. Will Queen Mary accept the children with an infectious disease? No good thinking about it.

St David's Society dinner for us. Those ruddy, friendly faces, those stocky figures and powerful rich voices. I feel at home among them. If only my headache would go. I swallow three aspirins.

Alan's speech is greeted with standing ovation. I congratulate him.

"Yes, it was very good," he states.

"Oh?" I think, cocky, isn't he? He laughs.

"It's a combination of Churchill, Eden and the Ambassador, so it has to be good!" Kind words all round. I bite my lip. I hate good-byes. Can't look at it as just a job.

Dining-room bursting with cutlery, china, linen, books, pictures — all ready for the packers. They move in. Dust, shavings, paper everywhere, and all over us. Then they're gone. We clear up. Pack personal belongings. Foam-cleaners move in. Now everything's clean, tidy, in place. Do the inventory.

Last parties. These made-up faces under ridiculous hats and loud voices, how dear they have become! I'll miss them; I'll miss them dreadfully. So many good-byes. I can't speak or I'll burst into tears.

We're ready and no measles.

Our last night. In bed I stare into the shadows. This flat, dark but spacious, where the children make faces at children in flats across the narrow street, and Alan has his own glass shower room; it's our home. We're continualy torn from home. I feel empty and cold inside.

"Alan," I murmur. "It's true what the French say, 'To leave is to die a little.'" He grunts. The night drags on.

I remember our arrival in New York. How vulgar and comic I thought Americans, lumping them together, judging from superficial appearances, so different from us. But then in these sophisticated Americans I sensed an innocence and cleanness, and through those endless cocktail parties and ceremonies, I glimpsed a miracle. I smile in the darkness. Yes, a miracle, this fusion of many different peoples pouring in from all over the world, our white Russian snobs included, all into one youthful, vital nation, bursting with energy and ideas, unlike us British fettered by tradition and precedent; and for every McCarthy there's sure to be a McCullough somewhere with a deep respect for the individual, white or black, and his right to go his own way. Now they're the leaders of the world — a pang shoots through me. It's no longer us but we must cling to them, use what influence we still have, keep their McCarthyites at bay with their communist threat paranoia. I doze off.

The Queen Mary. Our state room. Huge flower arrangements from friends and societies reflected in the numerous mirrors in the wood panelling. Family gathers round, smiling, keeping up a conversation. Mary and her Irish nannies in their best black coats, sniff into handkerchiefs, eyes red and swollen, while Kate, Ann and Barbara cling to them. Vania bounces our children on his knees, but half-heartedly. They clutch bars of chocolate but they

The family came to see us off

are quiet, troubled. Mamoo, her delicate features drawn, leans over him, holding tight to his shoulders. My sisters are silent, staring at us, watching our every movement. We drink champagne. My throat is tight. I try to smile. When shall we see them again? In another twenty years?

Alan is hearty, "Come on! Another round," and he refills glasses.

Then up on deck, searching for them in that seething, waving crowd below. Amidst hooting and shooting tugs edge us out of the dock, into the Hudson and out into the open sea. We're off. I cling to Alan's solid arm as we brave a fierce, cold wind and watch the battery skyline retreat. Spires shoot up from among solid, tall blocks, the slim silhouette of the Empire State Building soars high above them all and each skyscraper is etched sharply against the brilliant blue of the morning sky.

We're off.